Free Indeed

From the Book
of
Matthew Part I
(Message for Inspiration, Scriptures for
Meditation and Questions for Application)

Dr. Dorothy Batts

Permission forms are available by calling our administrative
office Monday-Thursday from 10:00 a.m. to 12:00 noon at
(910) 423-2999. Information will be sent to you free of charge.

Free Indeed

From the Book of Matthew Part I

Message for Inspiration, Scriptures for Meditation and Questions for Application

Copyright © 2014 by Dr. Dorothy Batts
ISBN: 978-0-9914246-6-5
First Edition
Printed in the United States of America

All scriptures taken from the King James Version of the Holy Bible

2 4 6 8 10 9 7 5 3 1

Cover design & layout by Bryan K. Reed - braynkreed.com
Edited by D. Renee Gibbs

Published by
Cranberry Quill Publishing, Inc.
111 Lamon Street, Suite 204, Fayetteville, NC 28301
www.CranberryQuill.com

TABLE OF CONTENTS

1	Introduction
7	Set Free
17	The Spirit of the Lord
35	Revelation Chapter 21 – Set Free from this Present Evil World, New Heaven and a New Earth
37	Revelation Chapter 22 – Surely I Come Quickly
39	Revelation Chapter 12:7-12 – The Kingdom of our God
41	Revelation Chapter 20 – They Shall be Priests of God and of Christ
43	But the Day of the Lord Will Come, The Lord is Not Slack Concerning His Promise
45	An In-depth Study of the Book of Matthew
46	Introduction – Prepare Ye The Way Of The Lord
49	Unto Christ are Fourteen Generations
55	Matthew Chapter 1 – Jesus' Earthly and Spiritual Generation, Emmanuel – God With us
60	Matthew Chapter 1 – Questions for Adults
62	Matthew Chapter 1 – Questions for Youth & Teens
63	Matthew Chapter 2 – Wise Men Come to Worship Jesus
68	Matthew Chapter 2 – Questions for Youth & Teens
70	Matthew Chapter 2 – Questions for Adults
73	Matthew Chapter 3 – Prepare Ye The Way of the Lord
79	Matthew Chapter 3 – Questions for Youth & Teens
80	Matthew Chapter 3 – Questions for Adults
83	Matthew Chapter 4 – The Lord Jesus Christ Tempted by the Devil
89	Jesus Christ Begins His Public Ministry
91	Matthew Chapter 4 – Questions for Adults
92	Matthew Chapter 4 – Questions for Youth & Teens
93	Matthew Chapter 5 – The Mountain Top Sermon
97	Matthew Chapter 5 – Questions for Youth & Teens
98	Matthew Chapter 5 – Questions for Adults
99	Matthew Chapter 6 – Your Motives When You Pray
103	Matthew Chapter 6 – Questions for Youth & Teens
104	Matthew Chapter 6 – Questions for Adults
105	Matthew Chapter 7 – Judge Not
110	Matthew Chapter 7 – Questions for Youth & Teens
111	Matthew Chapter 7 – Questions for Adults
113	Matthew Chapter 8 – King Jesus Has Power Over Defilement – Miracles Begin
117	Matthew Chapter 8 – Questions for Youth & Teens

118   Matthew Chapter 8 – Questions for Adults

119   Matthew Chapter 9 – That Ye May Know that the Son of Man Hath Power
        on Earth

124   Matthew Chapter 9 – Questions for Youth & Teens

125   Matthew Chapter 9 – Questions for Adults

127   Matthew Chapter 10 – He Had Called Unto Him His Twelve Disciples – The
        Kingdom of Heaven Is At Hand

132   Matthew Chapter 10 – Questions for Youth & Teens

133   Matthew Chapter 10 – Questions for Adults

135   Prepare Ye The Way of the Lord

136   Church Information

SET FREE

"He that the Son (Jesus Christ) set free is free indeed." (John 8:36)

Until the Lord returns, we have been given power by God to occupy until He comes. It does not matter how intense your battle might seem, God said we are overcomers. In Revelation 12:11, it reads, "And they overcame him by the blood of the Lamb, and by the word of their testimony; and they loved not their lives unto the death."

You have been set free if you are a child of the Most High God. Now, you must remain free. Do not allow yourself to become snared by the words of your mouth. Renew your mind with the gospel of Jesus Christ with the messages you will find in this book.

In the concluding chapters, you will find Jesus' teachings on the kingdom principles. Also, chapters and verses from Revelation to enlighten you on the destruction of the devil and the New Heaven and the New Earth.

"And I saw a new heaven and a new earth: for the first heaven and the first earth were passed away; and there was no more sea." (Revelation 21:1)

INTRODUCTION

John 8:30-36

"As he spake these words, many believed on him. Then said Jesus to those Jews which believed on him, If ye continue in my word, then are ye my disciples indeed; And ye shall know the truth, and the truth shall make you free. They answered him, We be Abraham's seed, and were never in bondage to any man: how sayest thou, Ye shall be made free? Jesus answered them, Verily, verily, I say unto you, Whosoever committeth sin is the servant of sin. And the servant abideth not in the house for ever: but the Son abideth ever. If the Son therefore shall make you free, ye shall be free indeed."

You have just received an impartation of present truth. Truth does not have power to become activated in your life unless you receive and believe the words you have just read and heard.

Your mind must become renewed with the Word of God. Until now, the devil has kept you in bondage with wrong thinking. If the thoughts you have had up until now did not agree with the Word of God, those thoughts were not of God; they were thoughts sent by the devil to bring you into bondage. You can say goodbye to all forms of bondage. This is your day of freedom. By the Word of God through the power and presence of the Holy Ghost, you will never be in bondage again. God does not lie.

He sent His Word to set you free and to bring healing to your spirit, soul and body. Yes, you have been hurt. Yes, you have been wounded by many words that came and pierced your heart. By the presence and the power of the blood of Jesus, you will never be the same again.

As you read those six verses in John 8:30-36, your healing begins. Almighty God said in Jeremiah 30:17 which reads, "For I will restore health unto thee, and I will heal thee of thy wounds, saith the LORD; because they called thee an Outcast, saying, This is Zion, whom no man seeketh after."

You have felt like an outcast and man might have looked at you as an outcast, but no more. Your days of being wounded and feeling like an outcast and your days of being in bondage are over. As you read and study the Word of God, you are being set free. Every wound you have received in the past, you are being healed and set free. It is written in Psalms 107:20, "He sent his word, and healed them, and delivered them from their destructions."

It is not God's will for any type of bondage to bind you. When you are bound, you are in a dark place. God will never leave you in a dark place of bondage. A dark place of bondage is any place you do not know how to get out of. Do not allow anything to keep your mind in a dark place of fear, sickness or oppression. God spoke and said in Psalms 107:14, "He brought them out of darkness and the shadow of death, and brake their bands in sunder."

You must realize there is no freedom outside of Jesus. If you have not received Jesus as Savior and Lord of your life, please do so before you go any further. All you need to do is say, "Jesus, I believe you are the Son of God. I believe you died on the cross for my sins. Now, I ask you to come into my heart. I receive you as my Savior and Lord. (Romans 10:8-11) Now fill me also with the power of Holy Spirit. (Acts 2:17-18) I believe you have saved me and I believe you have filled me with the Holy Ghost. I know I am in Christ and Christ Jesus is in me." (Colossians 1:27)

You are set free. Now, you are in Christ and Christ is in you. With the power of God in you, you have power to pull down strong holds and everything that exalts itself against the knowledge of God. Every thought that does not agree with God's Word are thoughts from the devil. They must be cast down.
It is so easy to become bound. I can understand why God moved upon the Apostle Paul to write these words in Galatians 5:16, "This I say then, Walk in the Spirit, and ye shall not fulfill the lust of the flesh."

To walk in the Spirit does not mean you will walk around speaking in tongues all day, (if the Holy Ghost come upon you to speak in tongues all day, do it), but to walk in the Spirit is to live a life style pleasing to

God. To live a life style pleasing to God is to obey His Word.

After you have been set free, you must remain free. In Galatians 5:1, we read, "Stand fast (That word "fast" simply means "to render secure and you will not be moved from the truth") therefore in the liberty wherewith Christ hath made us free, and be not entangled (That word "entangled" in the Greek translation is "buwk" which means "to be confused." Also, the word "enecho" which means "to keep a grade." Entanglement deals with the mind) again with the yoke of bondage."

Satan's objective is to keep you bound up in your mind with confusion. If he can keep your mind with confusion and carrying a grudge from the last person who hurt and offended you, he knows you will not be able to demonstrate the mind of Christ. He also knows if you are entangled with the facts, (facts deal with reason) but faith deals with the Word of God. To reason with facts will keep your mind confused. You need to have faith in God and believe every word He has spoken. Jesus came to set humanity free and bring us back to God. He brought us back to God free. He that the Son set free is free indeed.

You must learn to remain free. To remain free, you must know God's Word and have faith in the work of God. There is power in God's Word. When you are able to get God's Word from your head to your heart, the bondage of confusion will lose its hold on your mind. When truth can find an entrance, truth is on a commission by Christ. He is the Truth. Jesus is the Living Word of God. Jesus is seeking a place to enter in over through the bondages that has confused your mind and now you are set free. To know the truth is to understand and obey the truth.

In your walk with Christ, you must keep your thoughts lining up with the Word of God. Do not allow your mind to become confused. You must keep the mind of Christ.

If you are going to keep the mind of Christ, you must fortify yourself with prayer. Prayer is a command, it is not an option. All things are to be done by prayer and supplication. When you pray, the presence of God comes upon you. The power of Holy Spirit will give you the anointing to pull down the strong holds in your mind. You must have faith in God and believe when you pray. Your prayers are going out of your mouth and your prayers shall prevail over every thought that does not agree with God.

We have been anointed and appointed by God to root up and destroy every thought before that thought does not agree with God's Word to produce its fruit. The thoughts of your mind must be brought into captivity. When Jesus came into the world, He came to set us free and to demonstrate to us how sons of God were to live as free children of God.

After Jesus was baptized and the heavens were opened and the Spirit of the Lord came upon Him, He was led into the wilderness to be tempted by the devil. In the wilderness of temptation, which is a type and a shadow of the world we live in, is where the devil will try to place you in bondage. Jesus gives you the answer to remain free once you have become a child of God. Each time the devil came to bind up Jesus' mind with confusion, fear and temptations of this world; Jesus releases the weapon of God's Word. When Jesus said, "It is written", the Word of Jesus went out of His mouth like a two-edge sword. That Word began to cut every word away before it could get to Jesus. There is power in the Word of God.

That same Word that Jesus spoke with power and authority dwells in you. When the Word of God has renewed your mind, you will think like Christ did when the devil came to Him. I believe Jesus knew the devil will never have power to stop or destroy God's Word. He will come to hinder your prayers but he cannot stop God from answering your prayers. You are a child of the Most High God. You have been set free to learn how to live an abundant life that is governed by the Word of God. When you think like Christ, you are able to walk and talk like Christ.

When you walk and talk like Christ, you are Christ's living epistle being read by all men. The world needs to see how free children of God can live in this present world and not allow themselves to be control by the world's system. It is written in 1 John 5:4, " For whatsoever is born of God overcometh the world: and this is the victory that overcometh the world, even our faith."

You are born of God and God said, you are able to overcome the world. As I stated earlier and will repeat it again and again, the world is the bondages Satan will bring to your mind to try and get you to live a defeated Christian life, a life that is control by flesh. Jesus came so that you can be set free. You were translated out of this present evil world's system and you were translated into the kingdom of God's dear Son. As a son of God, you are empowered to overcome the word, the flesh and the devil as you renew your mind with the blood of Jesus and the power of the Holy Ghost. It is written in Hebrews 13:8, "Jesus Christ the same yesterday, and to day, and for ever."

In 1 John 5:4, John wrote, "For whatsoever is born of God overcometh the world: and this is the victory that overcometh the world, even our faith." Then John gives you a question and answers the question in the same sentence. In verse five, he writes, "Who is he that overcometh the world, but he that believeth that Jesus is the Son of God?"

In this message, God has blessed me to have it compiled into a book. It will empower and change your entire life as you apply the truth of God's Word.

SET FREE

John 8:32
"And ye shall know the truth, and the truth shall make you free."

It was about 6:00 a.m. and I had been lying in the bed meditating. I finally got on my knees to pray when I kept hearing the words, "Set Free." It did not take me long to remember that was the message the young man had preached the previous night under the anointing of God. The anointing was upon him and there was standing room only in my church.

There was such an impartation and revelation of present truth. I saw a manifestation of the presence and power of God. God spoke in my heart and said, "Dorothy, there are so many in the body of Christ that need to be set free. This is the last days and My Spirit is being poured out upon all flesh. They cannot prophesy by the Spirit unless they are set free in their spirit, soul and body. Freedom does not stop there; once they are Set Free, My people must be taught how to remain "Free Indeed."

I thought about The Emancipation Proclamation. The slaves were set free, but no one taught them how to remain free. Many slaves went back to their previous slave masters and became share croppers because no one taught them how to survive as a free man. They were never taught survival on how to begin with a new mind set. There is no new man without the man first having a renewed mind. The free slaves had to have their mind renewed so that they could think like a free man.

The free slaves begin to imitate the ways of a free man. They soon found out imitation without an impartation of a new mind was not a lasting thing. They reverted back to their old ways. The day came when the free slaves begin to be educated. They begin to read and write. Reading causes a part of their brain to be able to receive and process information. Being able to read also brought them into a place where they were able to dream; not only dreams of Freedom, but dreams of living a life of victory, peace and power. Their minds were becoming renewed. Their way of thinking began to change. They began to enjoy living like free men. Now, they must learn the laws and regulations of a man who has been set free.

Jesus said in Mark 8:34, "Whosoever will come after me, let him deny himself, and take up his cross, and follow me." He also said in Matthew 11:28, "Come unto me, all ye that labour and are heavy laden, and I will give you rest."

It does not matter who you are; lasting freedom only comes from Jesus. He gave an invitation to the world. He did not give that invitation with stipulation. He gave the invitation to every sinner. God demonstrated His love for us while we were yet sinners. In Romans 5:8, Paul wrote, "But God commendeth his love toward us, in that, while we were yet sinners, Christ died for us."

The demonstration of God's love for the world is spoken of in John 3:16-17 which reads…

> *"For God so loved the world, that he gave his only begotten Son, that whosoever believeth in him should not perish, but have everlasting life. For God sent not his Son into the world to condemn the world; but that the world through him might be saved."*

You were a slave to sin before you received Jesus Christ as Lord and Savior of your life. You lived your life in fear until you were set free. In Romans 8:15-17, we read…

> *"For ye have not received the spirit of bondage again to fear; but ye have received the Spirit of adoption, whereby we cry, Abba, Father. The Spirit itself beareth witness with our spirit, that we are the children of God: And if children, then heirs; heirs of God, and joint-heirs with Christ; if so be that we suffer with him, that we may be also glorified together."*

Now that you are in Christ, you are a child of God. You must renew your mind. If you do not change the way you think, you will remain a slave to your past. You cannot have a double mind. A double mind is the way you once thought when you were a slave to the world's way of thinking.

The world's way of thinking is any thoughts that do not agree with the Word of God. The Word of God regulates the kingdom of God. According to Romans 14:17, we read, "For the kingdom of God is not meat and drink; but righteousness, and peace, and joy in the Holy Ghost." Also, in Romans 4:20, we read, "For meat destroy not the work of God. All things indeed are pure; but it is evil for that man who eateth with offence." If the thoughts that come to your mind is not thoughts of righteousness, peace and joy in the Holy Ghost, then they are sent to you by the devil to bring you back into slavery.

You must ask yourself these three questions when a thought comes to your mind…

1. Is the thought going to assist you into right standards with Jesus?
2. Is the thought adding joy to my life? "…For the joy of the Lord is my strength." (Nehemiah 8:10b) If the thought causes any degree of fear, you must not allow that thought to take root. Paul told young Timothy in 2 Timothy 1:7, "For God hath not given us the spirit of fear; but of power, and of love, and of a sound mind."
3. A sound mind is a Christ-like mind. A kingdom mindset knows you have power, love and a sound mind. A sound mind is the mind of Christ.

When you received Jesus as Savior and Lord of your life, a translation took place. In Colossians 1:12, Paul gives a word of thanks to God for bringing us into the kingdom of God. We are children of King Jesus. Jesus is the King of kings. In Colossians 1:12-13, Paul wrote these words…

> *"Giving thanks unto the Father, which hath made us meet to be partakers of the inheritance of the saints in light: Who hath delivered us from the power of darkness, and hath translated (which means to cross over into the kingdom of God by the blood of Jesus and the power of the Holy Ghost) us into the kingdom of his dear Son."*

You must have faith in God and believe His Word. His Word plainly tells us we were translated into the kingdom of His dear Son. You must learn to live like a child of the King. The gospel of Jesus Christ along with the entire New Testament teaches us how to live the life of kings. Your power of darkness way of thinking must be done away with. You became a new creature in Christ when you were translated. Notice in 2 Corinthians 5:17, Paul writes, "Therefore if any man be in Christ, he is a new creature: old things are passed away; behold, all things are become new." You became a new creature in Christ, but you must renew your mind every day. You have been given the mind of Christ, but you must choose to "Let this mind be in you that was also in Christ Jesus." (Philippians 2:5)

When you were translated out of the powers of darkness, you put on the new man. That new man must have a new mind. In Colossians 3:10, it reads, "And have put on the new man, which is renewed in knowledge after the image of him that created him."

Through the knowledge of God's Word and the power of Holy Spirit, you will learn about King Jesus and the regulations that govern kingdom living. Your new man must learn God's new way of doing things. That new way is Jesus. He is the Way, the Truth and the Life of the Kingdom.

You are joint-heirs to Jesus Christ, who is the King of kings. When you were translated, you were also set free from the bondage of fear. The Spirit of God led you into freedom. In Romans 8:14-17, it reads…

> "For as many as are led by the Spirit of God, they are the sons of God. For ye have not received the spirit of bondage again to fear; but ye have received the Spirit of adoption, whereby we cry, Abba, Father. The Spirit itself beareth witness with our spirit, that we are the children of God: And if children, then heirs; heirs of God, and joint-heirs with Christ; if so be that we suffer with him, that we may be also glorified together."

As a child of God, you are a joint-heir with Christ. There will be times of suffering with Christ. You must not allow your season of suffering to cause you to forget who you are in Christ and whose you are. You are a child of the King. You must have faith in your God and boldly confess, "For I reckon that the sufferings of this present time are not worthy to be compared with the glory which shall be revealed in us." (Romans 8:18) There is no season of suffering that can out live your kingdom authority when you take your kingdom authority over that thing. There will be a revealing of the glory.

I believe the Apostle Paul must have experienced the glory of God after his season of suffering when he wrote in Colossians 1:12-17 these words…

> *"Giving thanks unto the Father, which hath made us meet to be partakers of the inheritance of the saints in light: Who hath delivered us from the power of darkness, and hath translated us into the kingdom of his dear Son: In whom we have redemption through his blood, even the forgiveness of sins: Who is the image of the invisible God, the firstborn of every creature: For by him were all things created, that are in heaven, and that are in earth, visible and invisible, whether they be thrones, or dominions, or principalities, or powers: all things were created by him, and for him: And he is before all things, and by him all things consist."*

Jesus is the image of the invisible God and we are to be conformed into the image of God's dear Son, Jesus. We were created by Him and we were created for Him. We are not our own. We have been bought with a price. That price was the blood of Jesus. Paul continues in verse 18, "And he is the head of the body, the church: who is the beginning, the firstborn from the dead; that in all things he might have the preeminence."

Jesus Christ is the head of the body, the church. The King, Jesus, is joined to us (the body of Christ, which is the church) and He is giving us the power we need to operate in kingship. You are not operating in your own power.

It is not by your power, neither is it by your might; but it is by the Spirit of God. When you operate in your kingdom authority, the devil sees you as a king. The same glory that is upon Jesus is also upon you. As you stand firm, rooted and grounded in your faith in God's Word, things that are not of God and does not agree with the Word of God; it shall bow.

You must have a renewed mind. If you do not renew your mind and have the mind of Christ in every situation, your words will not be with power and authority. In Philippians 2:5, we read, "Let this mind be in you, which was also in Christ Jesus." Jesus had the mind of a king and when He spoke, He spoke with power and authority. In Philippians 2:6-7, it reads…

> *"Who, being in the form of God, thought it not robbery to be equal with God: But made himself of no reputation, and took upon him the form of a servant, and was made in the likeness of men."*

Jesus is equal with God. We are not equal with Jesus, but we are joined to Him. What flows through Him also flows to us and through us. We could boldly and humbly say decree Romans 8:10-11 which reads…

> *"And if Christ be in you, the body is dead because of sin; but the Spirit is life because of righteousness. But if the Spirit of him that raised up Jesus from the dead dwell in you, he that raised up Christ from the dead shall also quicken your mortal bodies by his Spirit that dwelleth in you."*

He that raised Christ from the dead dwell in us. As you speak by the power and authority of God's Word, things begin to happen in the heavens and in the earth when the name of Jesus is released. Paul being inspired by the Holy Ghost revealed to us what takes place at the name of Jesus. In Philippians 2:9-11 we read…

"Wherefore God also hath highly exalted him, and given him a name which is above every name: That at the name of Jesus every knee should bow, of things in heaven, and things in earth, and things under the earth; And that every tongue should confess that Jesus Christ is Lord, to the glory of God the Father."

If the devil can keep you in bondage with a slave mentality, you will never experience total freedom. This is the acceptable year of the Lord. The year of the redeemed of the Lord. The year when God's will is being done in the earth by those who are willing to make a sacrifice for the Savior and follow the example of Jesus.

Jesus told us in John 10:10, "The thief cometh not, but for to steal, and to kill, and to destroy: I am come that they might have life, and that they might have it more abundantly." He comes to steal your faith in the Word of God and impart a spirit of fear in your mind. He does not want you to believe you are a son of God and a joint-heir with Jesus Christ. The devil knows if you believe, Jesus came to set you free from the spirit of fear and free from the powers of darkness. You are a new creation. Now, you must learn how to remain free.

God has given us the way to remain free. The way is Jesus. In John 14:6, Jesus said, "Jesus saith unto him, I am the way, the truth, and the life: no man cometh unto the Father, but by me." You must learn to apply the Word of God to your daily life. God said in Isaiah 55:11, "So shall my word be that goeth forth out of my mouth: it shall not return unto me void, but it shall accomplish that which I please, and it shall prosper in the thing whereto I sent it."

The Word of God has gone out of the mouth of God and His Word must do what God has assigned it to do. When the Word of God goes out of the mouth of God, there has to be a corresponding action in the earth. The children of God must receive and believe the Word that has come out of the mouth of God. There is power in agreement.

God has allowed holy men of God to write the words that came out of the mouth of God. These words God spoke are written in the Bible. God did not stop with the written Word, but God loved us so much until His Word became flesh and dwelled among the people in the earth at that time. Not only did the Word of God become flesh to reveal to us the mind of God, but the Word of God was the only begotten Son of God who was going to die on the cross for the sins of the world. The Word of God, who is Jesus Christ, died on the cross, was buried and on the third day He rose from the dead.

Jesus Christ went into the earth and He set the captives free. In Ephesians 4:8-10, we read…

> *"Wherefore he saith, When he ascended up on high, he led captivity captive, and gave gifts unto men. (Now that he ascended, what is it but that he also descended first into the lower parts of the earth?,He that descended is the same also that ascended up far above all heavens, that he might fill all things.)"*

Jesus Christ, the Son of God, came to set the captives free. It does not matter what name has been given to the thing that has you in bondage; this is a new day. This is your day for victory. When Jesus went down into the grave, the Word of God does not say He fought with the devil. I believe the devil knew better than to show up in the lower parts of the earth while Jesus, the living Word of God, was there.

When Lucifer was in heaven and tried to over throw God, he was thrown out of heaven like lighting. In Luke 10:17, Luke wrote of the beginning of Satan's overthrow which reads…

> *"And the seventy returned again with joy, saying, Lord, even the devils are subject unto us through thy name. And he said unto them, I beheld Satan as lightning fall from heaven."*

Then Jesus spoke of every believer's victory through Jesus Christ. The devil is not going to give up without a struggle. As I stated earlier, he comes to steal, kill and destroy. You must have faith in the Word of God and believe every word that proceeds out of the mouth of God.

These words came out of the mouth of God and God does not lie. In Luke 10:19, Jesus said, "Behold, I give unto you power to tread on serpents and scorpions, and over all the power of the enemy: and nothing shall by any means hurt you." We have been given power over all the power of the enemy. Notice, Jesus called him the enemy. You are to view him as your enemy. He goes around as a roaring lion seeking whom he may devour.

Jesus has already revealed to us the outcome of every battle. Our attitude should be that of one who believes we are more than a conqueror through Him that loved us. Paul lists the things that Satan will try to cause you to become weary in your faith. You must hold fast to the confession of your faith without wavering, for He is a faithful God who promised He will never fail you.

The Apostle Paul begins with a question. "Who shall separate us from the love of Christ?" Whatever you love, you are waiting to die for. That is exactly what Jesus did. He demonstrated His love for us while we were yet sinners. It is written in Romans 5:6-11, which reads…

> *"For when we were yet without strength, in due time Christ died for the ungodly. For scarcely for a righteous man will one die: yet peradventure for a good man some would even dare to die. But God commendeth his love toward us, in that, while we were yet sinners, Christ died for us. Much more then, being now justified by his blood, we shall be saved from wrath through him. For if, when we were enemies, we were reconciled to God by the death of his Son, much more, being reconciled, we shall be saved by his life. And not only so, but we also joy in God through our Lord Jesus Christ, by whom we have now received the atonement."*

Your position is in Christ. Your power is coming from Christ. Your victory was pre-ordained by our Lord Jesus Christ. You must believe you are more than a conqueror while you are in the midst of a battle and it looks as if you are fighting alone. Keep renewing your mind with these words from Hebrew 13:5-6 which reads…

> *"Let your conversation be without covetousness; and be content with such things as ye have: for he hath said, I will never leave thee, nor forsake thee. So that we may boldly say, The Lord is my helper, and I will not fear what man shall do unto me."*

God said, "I will never leave you and I will not forsake you." When you have faith in God, you must not allow the devil to sow a seed of fear. You must choose to trust God. There are many things in this world we will never understand. God told us what we are to do when we cannot understand the tribulation in the world today.

The Word of God tells us in Proverbs 3:5, that we are to "Trust in the LORD with all thine heart; and lean not unto thine own understanding." You must elevate your mind. As you study the Word of God and believe what God's Word is saying, your mind is becoming elevated. When you have the mind of Christ, you can boldly say, "In God have I put my trust: I will not be afraid what man can do unto me." (Psalms 56:11)

THE SPIRIT OF THE LORD

Luke 4:18-19
"The Spirit of the Lord is upon me, because he hath anointed me to preach the gospel to the poor; he hath sent me to heal the brokenhearted, to preach deliverance to the captives, and recovering of sight to the blind, to set at liberty them that are bruised, To preach the acceptable year of the Lord."

Jesus said in Matthew 16:24b, "…Follow Me." Every step Jesus took led to freedom. If you follow Jesus, you will never be bound again.

You cannot follow man and remain free. You must choose to walk in the Spirit and do not fulfill the lust of the flesh. Do you know what the flesh is?

To walk in the flesh is to disobey the Word of God you know. God is so good until He will make sure you hear the Word of God when you desire to be set free.

When you choose to walk in the flesh, the works of the flesh will bind you up. There are too many in the body of Christ who were once set free but now they are bound up again. They gave place to the devil. Anytime you give place to the devil, he will take that opportunity to bind up your mind first so that you will not have the mind of Christ.

Today, the voice of God is coming to you. God said in Hebrews 3:15, "While it is said, To day if ye will hear his voice, harden not your hearts, as in the provocation." The voice of the Lord, through the Word and the Spirit of God, is coming to you this day and the Spirit of the Lord is loosing you from every bondage. Now, follow Jesus! As long as you follow Jesus, you will live a life of victory, peace and power.

I did not say you would never again experience tribulation. Jesus said in John 16:33, "…In the world you shall have tribulation…" As long as this present evil world is here, you shall have tribulation; but you are never to allow tribulation to trouble you. Jesus said, "…Be of good cheer for I have overcome the world." You must remind yourself when the adversaries of life try to bind you up again, "Speak to yourself and tell yourself I am following Jesus. I will never be bound again. Tribulation will come my way, but I have prepared myself for victory by renewing my mind with the Word of God and walking in the Spirit." "It is the spirit that quickeneth; the flesh profiteth nothing: the words that I speak unto you, they are spirit, and they are life." (John 6:63)

You have the Spirit of the living God in you. Christ in you is the hope of glory. The glory of God is the quickening power of God in you and upon you to quicken you so that you will never be bound again.

Just as the Spirit of the Lord was upon Jesus and He was anointed to preach or proclaim the gospel, the Spirit of the Lord is upon you. The devil will try to get you to believe you must live the rest of your life bound to the works of the flesh. Don't allow him to use you as a carrier of his evil devices. Learn to recognize the works of the flesh. Why do you need to be able to detect the works of the flesh? Anything you are able to detect, you have the power of God to destroy that thing.

In Galatians 5:17, the Word of God reads, "For the flesh lusteth against the Spirit, and the Spirit against the flesh: and these are contrary the one to the other: so that ye cannot do the things that ye would."

The works of the flesh are manifest or made known to you so that you can detect them when they try to show up and you have been given the power of God, which is the Spirit of God upon you, so that you can destroy them. You must know that in your flesh dwells no good thing, but you have been given power to destroy every evil work of the devil.

Every creature was born in sin and shaped in iniquity. Due to the sin of Adam and Eve, sin was passed down to the entire human race. It was not God's perfect will for mankind to live in a world outside of the presence of God. God is a holy God and no sin can dwell in His presence. God's perfect will for mankind is found in Genesis 1:26-28, which reads…

"And God said, Let us make man in our image, after our likeness: and let them have dominion over the fish of the sea, and over the fowl of the air, and over the cattle, and over all the earth, and over every creeping thing that creepeth upon the earth. So God created man in his own image, in the image of God created he him; male and female created he them. And God blessed them, and God said unto them, Be fruitful, and multiply, and replenish the earth, and subdue it: and have dominion over the fish of the sea, and over the fowl of the air, and over every living thing that moveth upon the earth."

Mankind was created in the image and likeness of God, "Free." Eve allowed the devil, in the form of a snack, to deceive her and she disobeyed the commandment of God. After Eve became deceived, she also deceived Adam and he also disobeyed God. Adam and Eve became bound by the sin of deception. Anytime you disobey God, you will become bound.

In Genesis 3:23-24, we read of Adam and Eve being driven out of the presence of God. Out of God's presence, they had to make decisions for themselves. Their decisions would either determine their liberty or their bondage. They had learned a valuable lesson while they were in the Garden of Eden. The lesson Adam and Eve learned was that disobedience comes with a price. While they were in the garden, God had made all the decisions for them. They were in God's presence continually.

God met with them in the cool of the day, but the presence of God never left them. Once the seed of sin entered Adam and Eve, they became separated from the presence of God. God called out to Adam and Eve and said, "Where are you?" Adam and Eve became bound in condemnation. They were hiding from the presence of God. Instead of coming out of hiding and asking God to forgive them and be set free, they tried to cover up the thing that had them in bondage.

When God came in contact with Adam and Eve, He told them the penalty of sin. When God shed blood so that they could be covered in their sinful state, it was a type and shadow of Jesus coming into the world in the fullness of time and shedding His blood for the sins of the world. In Genesis 3:24, the Lord came upon Moses and he wrote the exodus of Adam and Eve being driven out of the presence of God. It reads, "So he drove out the man; and he placed at the east of the garden of Eden Cherubims, and a flaming sword which turned every way, to keep the way of the tree of life."

In Genesis 4:8, we read of Cain being in bondage with the Spirit of jealousy. Jealousy is a word of the flesh. All works of the flesh are ropes the devil will use to keep you in bondage. Believe it or not, all works of the flesh begin with a thought in your mind. You must learn to detect and destroy every imagination and every high thing that exalts itself against the knowledge of God and you must bring every thought into the obedience of Christ.

The Apostle Paul spoke with boldness, confidence and faith in the Lord Jesus Christ when he spoke these words in 2 Corinthians 10:3-5…

> "For though we walk in the flesh, we do not war after the flesh: (For the weapons of our warfare are not carnal, but mighty through God to the pulling down of strong holds;) Casting down imaginations, and every high thing that exalteth itself against the knowledge of God, and bringing into captivity every thought to the obedience of Christ."

It is not the work of the flesh you are warring after; it is the thoughts the devil put in your mind. The mind of man is the soulish realm. The mind of Christ is the Spirit of Christ dwelling in you and flowing through you. "…Christ in you, the hope of glory." (Colossians 1:27)

God has given you power through Holy Spirit, the blood of Jesus and the Word of God to pull down the strongholds of your mind. In 2 Corinthians 10:4-6, Paul writes these words…

> "(For the weapons of our warfare are not carnal, but mighty through God to the pulling down of strong holds;) Casting down imaginations, and every high thing that exalteth itself against the

20

knowledge of God, and bringing into captivity every thought to the obedience of Christ; And having in a readiness to revenge all disobedience, when your obedience is fulfilled."

You might think I am being repetitious when I repeat the same statement over and over again. It is not a typographical error; I am being led by Holy Spirit. The Lord knows the areas of your life you are having struggles with and you have not received faith to be set free and remain free. Many get free but they do not have the faith in God to remain free.

The Word of God tells us in Romans 10:17, "So then faith cometh by hearing, and hearing by the word of God." That means you must hear God's Word over and over again and again until you know you will never be in bondage again with that one thing. You will also become spiritually and emotionally empowered with the Word of God so that you will prophesy to yourself with these words, "I am anointed of God and I am "Casting down imaginations, and every high thing that exalteth itself against the knowledge of God, and bringing into captivity every thought to the obedience of Christ." (2 Corinthians 10:5)

Imaginations are the images the devil puts in your mind. Every thought that does not agree with the Word of God needs to be cast down immediately. My husband use to say, "Don't toy with temptation." In other words he was saying, "Don't play around with the thoughts the devil will try to bring to your mind."

You have been given power by God to throw those thoughts out of your mind as far as the north is from the south and the east is from the west. If you will bring every thought into the obedience of Christ, you will never allow the devil to use your mind as his avenue to carry out his wicked plans.

He used the mind of Cain. Cain thought God honored Abel's offering more than his offering. He became so bound up with the thoughts of rejection until he killed his brother Abel. When Adam and Eve left the presence of God, the presence of God must have remained with them. We find God communicating with Cain in Genesis 4:16 which reads, "And Cain went out from the presence of the LORD, and dwelt in the land of Nod, on the east of Eden."

We see a manifestation of God's great love being shown to Cain in Genesis 4:10-15. Cain went out of the presence of the Lord, but he did not leave in bondage. God set a mark upon him. How great is God's grace and mercy to us. What a great and mighty God we serve. You must fill your mind and your heart with the Word of God. God loves you so much until He manifested the works of the flesh in Galatians 5:19-21 which reads…

> "Now the works of the flesh are manifest, which are these; Adultery, fornication, uncleanness, lasciviousness, Idolatry, witchcraft, hatred, variance, emulations, wrath, strife, seditions, heresies, Envyings, murders, drunkenness, revellings, and such like: of the which I tell you before, as I have also told you in time past, that they which do such things shall not inherit the kingdom of God."

You are given a command to "…Walk in the Spirit, and ye shall not fulfill the lust of the flesh." (Galatians 5:16)

Your mind will try and convince you to obey the imaginations the devil has brought to your mind. You cast them down. The devil is not going to leave unless you begin manifesting the fruit of the Spirit. Just as you know what the works of the flesh are; you need to know and manifest the fruit of the Spirit.

Don't allow the devil to cause you to fear. You can do all things through Christ. It does not matter how many times you tried to please God in the past and failed; today is a new day. God is so good and our God is so wise. He called His attribute the fruit of the Spirit. The harvest of fruit is not grown overnight. The seed of God's Word must first be sown by God's anointed men and women.

There is a process every seed of God's Word must go through before it becomes rooted and grounded in your heart. When you hear the Word of God, that Word enters your mind. As you receive the Word of God in your mind, that anointed Word begins to destroy every stronghold and every high thing that exalts itself against the knowledge of God.

Your mind is being set free by the blood of the Lamb and the Word of God. You begin to have faith in the Word that has cast down imaginations. Once your mind has been set free, the Word of God enters into your heart. You can boldly decree as David did in Psalms 119:11, "Thy word have I hid in mine heart, that I might not sin against thee."

The seed of God's Word has taken root. Now, it will produce the fruit of the Spirit. You will realize, "It is no more I, but Christ." When you feel as if you have missed the mark and you did not produce the fruit of the Spirit in a certain situation, you will not allow yourself to become bound with condemnation. You will ask God to forgive you, believe Jesus' blood has cleansed you and you will renew your mind with 1 John 2:1 which reads, "My little children, these things write I unto you, that ye sin not. And if any man sin, we have an advocate with the Father, Jesus Christ the righteous."

An "advocate" is like an attorney who pleads your case in court. Your Advocate is Jesus Christ who is the "Atonement" for the sins of the world. He shed His blood as payment for the sins of the world. Jesus is our "Advocate" in heaven and he pled our case before God. He did not leave us without an advocate in the earth. According to John 14:16-17, 26; 15:26 and 16:7, the comforter, who is the Holy Ghost, has been sent to be our "Advocate" in the earth.

Now, you can boldly decree, "There is therefore now no condemnation to them which are in Christ Jesus, who walk not after the flesh, but after the Spirit." (Romans 8:1)

Now, the Apostle Paul writes in Galatians 5:22-23…

> "But the fruit of the Spirit is love, joy, peace, longsuffering, gentleness, goodness, faith, Meekness, temperance: against such there is no law."

This is the day when you must examine yourself to check yourself out to see if you are in the faith. When you are in the faith of our Lord Jesus Christ, you will be empowered by Jesus to love without limits. It is not by your strength neither is it by your power you are able to love without limits. You are divinely connected to the vine, who is Jesus, and His power is flowing through you, who are the branch.

It is impossible to love without limits unless you remain connected to the vine. It is not your faith you are living by every minute of the day; it is the faith of the Lord Jesus Christ. The Apostle Paul wrote these words after he had learned to live by the faith of our Lord Jesus Christ. In Galatians 2:20, he wrote these words to us, " I am crucified with Christ: nevertheless I live; yet not I, but Christ liveth in me: and the life which I now live in the flesh I live by the faith of the Son of God, who loved me, and gave himself for me."

Keep in mind, dead men don't move. If you are allowing the words and the reactions of man to keep you in the bondage of hurt, anger and fear; you are not dead yet. Examine yourself. Until you come to that place in God where you know and believe you are divinely attached to Jesus, you will remain bound.

If you find yourself constantly saying, "They hurt me; they did me wrong; they should be dealt with; I will not allow them to do me like that; I know this is not God's will and God is going to get them." Don't get angry with me when I tell you, you have allowed the power of man to put you in bondage and until you are set free, you will never be able to love without limits. You are allowing the power of man to keep you in bondage under his control. Anytime your joy, peace and victory depend on anyone except Jesus; you will remain in bondage until Jesus returns. Notice, I did not say you were not saved neither did I say you were not a spirit-filled child of God; I simply said, you are living a life bound by man when you depend on your husband, wife, children, relatives, friends, employer, money or the system of this present world to give you joy.

It is God's perfect will that you receive joy everyday of your life. It is not the happiness of man that will bring you the strength you will need to face the adversities of life; but it is the joy that only comes from the Lord, who is the Master of your life. You must learn to look to Jesus. When you keep your eyes on Jesus, you will remain divinely attached to the vine and you will be able to say, "It is not more I, but Christ."

A crucified life is a life that has been crucified. One crucifixion does not do it. We are being crucified all the day long, everyday of our lives. Learn to recognize any area in your life you have not been crucified in. When the words someone has said to you or their actions towards you have caused you to feel like "it hurts to hurt," you know you are not totally dead in that area of your life and you need to set your eyes on Jesus. I feel led of the Lord to pray for every Spirit-filled believer who has come to that place in your life where you feel as if, "it hurts to hurt." When you come to that place where it "hurts to hurt," you are tired of hurting and you have told yourself it does not look as if you are receiving results, even though you are praying, fasting and confessing the Word of God.

You have come to the conclusion you will begin to exist instead of living an abundant Christian life of joy and peace divinely connected to the vine. This is not God's divine plan for your life. His plan is that you come to that place He has chosen for you as you remain divinely attached to the vine. You must learn to draw from Jesus and live a crucified life by Him and through Him.

Now, in the name of Jesus Christ, the Son of the Living God; I speak by the Holy Spirit into your life. I take authority in the name of Jesus Christ, the Son of the Living God, over every word that has been spoken into your life to hurt, discourage and wound you. I command their words and their actions to be destroyed by the blood of Jesus and the Word of God. The years of abuse with their words, the years of hurt and pain that brought you into a prison; God has seen your pain and God has heard your cries and He has sent deliverance to your spirit, soul and body. Be healed and set free in Jesus' Name. Be healed and set free to love without limits. Be healed and set free and receive the power to be crucified each day. Be healed in the name of Jesus for the blood of Jesus is washing you of the years of hurt and pain. The blood of Jesus has re-attached you to the vine and you are receiving joy and peace in the Holy Ghost. You have been set free and "He that the Son Set Free is Free Indeed!"

Every time you need the healing power of Jesus to heal your wounded spirit, read and meditate upon this prayer day and night along with your daily Bible reading during your time of Bible Study. I believe God will give you what you need each day to enjoy the rest of your life free of the opinions and hurt that come from people. God loves you. You were created for His divine purpose. The fruit of "Love" is being grown in and through your life. The Word of God reads in Galatians 5:22-23…

> "But the fruit of the Spirit is love, joy, peace, longsuffering, gentleness, goodness, faith, Meekness, temperance: against such there is no law."

The Apostle Paul concludes with these words in verse 24, "And they that are Christ's have crucified the flesh with the affections and lusts."

It is impossible to love without limits unless you love through a life that has been crucified. You must live in the Spirit. In Galatians 5:26, Paul writes, "Let us not be desirous of vain glory, provoking one another, envying one another."

YOU HAVE BEEN SET FREE BY OUR
LORD AND SAVIOR JESUS CHRIST

Through God's love, grace, mercy and His Word, you will learn how to live as sons of God and joint heirs to Jesus Christ. Your life as a child of the king began when you received Jesus as Savior and Lord of your life. Your kingdom authority began when you received Jesus as Savior and Lord of your life. You asked God to fill you with the Holy Ghost. You have power to live your life by the instructions given to us by Jesus in Matthew chapters 5-7. Read, meditate and apply the principles of the kingdom.

GOD'S PRINCIPLES OF THE KINGDOM
(Matthew Chapter 5)

"And seeing the multitudes, he went up into a mountain: and when he was set, his disciples came unto him: And he opened his mouth, and taught them, saying, Blessed are the poor in spirit: for theirs is the kingdom of heaven. Blessed are they that mourn: for they shall be comforted. Blessed are the meek: for they shall inherit the earth. Blessed are they which do hunger and thirst after righteousness: for they shall be filled. Blessed are the merciful: for they shall obtain mercy. Blessed are the pure in heart: for they shall see God. Blessed are the peacemakers: for they shall be called the children of God. Blessed are they which are persecuted for righteousness' sake: for theirs is the kingdom of heaven. Blessed are ye, when men shall revile you, and persecute you, and shall say all manner of evil against you falsely, for my sake. Rejoice, and be exceeding glad: for great is your reward in heaven: for so persecuted they the prophets which were before you. Ye are the salt of the earth: but if the salt have lost his savour, wherewith shall it be salted? it is thenceforth good for nothing, but to be cast out, and to be trodden under foot of men. Ye are the light of the world. A city that is set on an hill cannot be hid. Neither do men light a candle, and put it under a bushel, but on a candlestick; and it giveth light unto all that are in the house. Let your light so shine before men, that they may see your good works, and glorify your Father which is in heaven. Think not that I am come to destroy the law, or the prophets: I am not come to destroy, but to fulfil. For verily I say unto you, Till heaven

and earth pass, one jot or one tittle shall in no wise pass from the law, till all be fulfilled. Whosoever therefore shall break one of these least commandments, and shall teach men so, he shall be called the least in the kingdom of heaven: but whosoever shall do and teach them, the same shall be called great in the kingdom of heaven. For I say unto you, That except your righteousness shall exceed the righteousness of the scribes and Pharisees, ye shall in no case enter into the kingdom of heaven. Ye have heard that it was said by them of old time, Thou shalt not kill; and whosoever shall kill shall be in danger of the judgment: But I say unto you, That whosoever is angry with his brother without a cause shall be in danger of the judgment: and whosoever shall say to his brother, Raca, shall be in danger of the council: but whosoever shall say, Thou fool, shall be in danger of hell fire. Therefore if thou bring thy gift to the altar, and there rememberest that thy brother hath ought against thee; Leave there thy gift before the altar, and go thy way; first be reconciled to thy brother, and then come and offer thy gift. Agree with thine adversary quickly, whiles thou art in the way with him; lest at any time the adversary deliver thee to the judge, and the judge deliver thee to the officer, and thou be cast into prison. Verily I say unto thee, Thou shalt by no means come out thence, till thou hast paid the uttermost farthing. Ye have heard that it was said by them of old time, Thou shalt not commit adultery: But I say unto you, That whosoever looketh on a woman to lust after her hath committed adultery with her already in his heart. And if thy right eye offend thee, pluck it out, and cast it from thee: for it is profitable for thee that one of thy members should perish, and not that thy whole body should be cast into hell. And if thy right hand offend thee, cut if off, and cast it from thee: for it is profitable for thee that one of thy members should perish, and not that thy whole body should be cast into hell. It hath been said, Whosoever shall put away his wife, let him give her a writing of divorcement: But I say unto you, That whosoever shall put away his wife, saving for the cause of fornication, causeth her to commit adultery: and whosoever shall marry her that is divorced committeth adultery. Again, ye have heard that it hath been said by them of old time, Thou shalt not forswear thyself, but shalt perform unto the Lord thine oaths: But I say unto you, Swear not at all; neither by heaven; for it is God's throne: Nor by the earth; for it is his footstool: neither by Jerusalem; for it is the city of the great King. Neither shalt thou swear by thy head, because thou canst not make one hair white or black. But let *your communication be, Yea, yea; Nay, nay: for whatsoever is more than these cometh of evil. Ye have heard that it hath been said, An eye for an eye, and a tooth for a tooth: But I say unto you, That ye resist not evil: but whosoever shall smite thee on thy right cheek, turn to him the other also. And if any man will sue thee at the law, and take away thy coat, let him have thy cloke also. And whosoever shall compel thee to go a mile, go with him twain. Give to him that asketh thee, and from him that would borrow of thee turn not thou away. Ye have heard that it hath been said, Thou shalt love thy neighbour, and hate thine enemy. But I say unto you, Love your enemies, bless them that curse you, do good to them that hate you, and pray for them which despitefully use you, and persecute you; That ye may be the children of your Father which is in heaven: for he maketh his sun to rise on the evil and on the good, and sendeth rain on the just and on the unjust. For if ye love them which love you, what reward have ye? do not even the publicans the same? And if ye salute your brethren only, what do ye more than others? do not even the publicans so? Be ye therefore perfect, even as your Father which is in heaven is perfect."*

MATTHEW CHAPTER 6

"Take heed that ye do not your alms before men, to be seen of them: otherwise ye have no reward of your Father which is in heaven. Therefore when thou doest thine alms, do not sound a trumpet before thee, as the hypocrites do in the synagogues and in the streets, that they may have glory of men. Verily I say unto you, They have their reward. But when thou doest alms, let not thy left hand know what thy right hand doeth: That thine alms may be in secret: and thy Father which seeth in secret himself shall reward thee openly. And when thou prayest, thou shalt not be as the hypocrites are: for they love to pray standing in the synagogues and in the corners of the streets, that they may be seen of men. Verily I say unto you, They have their reward. But thou, when thou prayest, enter into thy closet, and when thou hast shut thy door, pray to thy Father which is in secret; and thy Father which seeth in secret shall reward thee openly. But when ye pray, use not vain repetitions, as the heathen do: for they think that they shall be heard for their much speaking. Be not ye therefore like unto them: for your Father knoweth what things ye have need of, before ye ask

him. After this manner therefore pray ye: Our Father which art in heaven, Hallowed be thy name. Thy kingdom come. Thy will be done in earth, as it is in heaven. Give us this day our daily bread. And forgive us our debts, as we forgive our debtors. And lead us not into temptation, but deliver us from evil: For thine is the kingdom, and the power, and the glory, for ever. Amen. For if ye forgive men their trespasses, your heavenly Father will also forgive you: But if ye forgive not men their trespasses, neither will your Father forgive your trespasses. Moreover when ye fast, be not, as the hypocrites, of a sad countenance: for they disfigure their faces, that they may appear unto men to fast. Verily I say unto you, They have their reward. But thou, when thou fastest, anoint thine head, and wash thy face; That thou appear not unto men to fast, but unto thy Father which is in secret: and thy Father, which seeth in secret, shall reward thee openly. Lay not up for yourselves treasures upon earth, where moth and rust doth corrupt, and where thieves break through and steal: But lay up for yourselves treasures in heaven, where neither moth nor rust doth corrupt, and where thieves do not break through nor steal: For where your treasure is, there will your heart be also. The light of the body is the eye: if therefore thine eye be single, thy whole body shall be full of light. But if thine eye be evil, thy whole body shall be full of darkness. If therefore the light that is in thee be darkness, how great is that darkness! No man can serve two masters: for either he will hate the one, and love the other; or else he will hold to the one, and despise the other. Ye cannot serve God and mammon. Therefore I say unto you, Take no thought for your life, what ye shall eat, or what ye shall drink; nor yet for your body, what ye shall put on. Is not the life more than meat, and the body than raiment? Behold the fowls of the air: for they sow not, neither do they reap, nor gather into barns; yet your heavenly Father feedeth them. Are ye not much better than they? Which of you by taking thought can add one cubit unto his stature? And why take ye thought for raiment? Consider the lilies of the field, how they grow; they toil not, neither do they spin: And yet I say unto you, That even Solomon in all his glory was not arrayed like one of these. Wherefore, if God so clothe the grass of the field, which to day is, and to morrow is cast into the oven, shall he not much more clothe you, O ye of little faith? Therefore take no thought, saying, What shall we eat? or, What shall we drink? or, Wherewithal shall we be clothed? (For after all these things do the Gentiles seek:) for your heavenly Father knoweth that ye have need of all these things.

But seek ye first the kingdom of God, and his righteousness; and all these things shall be added unto you. Take therefore no thought for the morrow: for the morrow shall take thought for the things of itself. Sufficient unto the day is the evil thereof."

MATTHEW CHAPTER 7

"Judge not, that ye be not judged. For with what judgment ye judge, ye shall be judged: and with what measure ye mete, it shall be measured to you again. And why beholdest thou the mote that is in thy brother's eye, but considerest not the beam that is in thine own eye? Or how wilt thou say to thy brother, Let me pull out the mote out of thine eye; and, behold, a beam is in thine own eye? Thou hypocrite, first cast out the beam out of thine own eye; and then shalt thou see clearly to cast out the mote out of thy brother's eye. Give not that which is holy unto the dogs, neither cast ye your pearls before swine, lest they trample them under their feet, and turn again and rend you. Ask, and it shall be given you; seek, and ye shall find; knock, and it shall be opened unto you: For every one that asketh receiveth; and he that seeketh findeth; and to him that knocketh it shall be opened. Or what man is there of you, whom if his son ask bread, will he give him a stone? Or if he ask a fish, will he give him a serpent? If ye then, being evil, know how to give good gifts unto your children, how much more shall your Father which is in heaven give good things to them that ask him? Therefore all things whatsoever ye would that men should do to you, do ye even so to them: for this is the law and the prophets. Enter ye in at the strait gate: for wide is the gate, and broad is the way, that leadeth to destruction, and many there be which go in thereat: Because strait is the gate, and narrow is the way, which leadeth unto life, and few there be that find it. Beware of false prophets, which come to you in sheep's clothing, but inwardly they are ravening wolves. Ye shall know them by their fruits. Do men gather grapes of thorns, or figs of thistles? Even so every good tree bringeth forth good fruit; but a corrupt tree bringeth forth evil fruit. A good tree cannot bring forth evil fruit, neither can a corrupt tree bring forth good fruit. Every tree that bringeth not forth good fruit is hewn down, and cast into the fire. Wherefore by their fruits ye shall know them. Not every one that saith unto me, Lord, Lord, shall enter into the kingdom of heaven; but he that doeth the will of my Father which is in heaven. Many

will say to me in that day, Lord, Lord, have we not prophesied in thy name? and in thy name have cast out devils? and in thy name done many wonderful works? And then will I profess unto them, I never knew you: depart from me, ye that work iniquity. Therefore whosoever heareth these sayings of mine, and doeth them, I will liken him unto a wise man, which built his house upon a rock: And the rain descended, and the floods came, and the winds blew, and beat upon that house; and it fell not: for it was founded upon a rock. And every one that heareth these sayings of mine, and doeth them not, shall be likened unto a foolish man, which built his house upon the sand: And the rain descended, and the floods came, and the winds blew, and beat upon that house; and it fell: and great was the fall of it. And it came to pass, when Jesus had ended these sayings, the people were astonished at his doctrine: For he taught them as one having authority, and not as the scribes."

The kingdom of God is within you. The Apostle Paul writes in 1 Thessalonians 4:1, "Furthermore then we beseech you, brethren, and exhort you by the Lord Jesus, that as ye have received of us how ye ought to walk and to please God, so ye would abound more and more."

Also, in 1 Thessalonians 4:13-18, Paul continues…

"But I would not have you to be ignorant, brethren, concerning them which are asleep, that ye sorrow not, even as others which have no hope. For if we believe that Jesus died and rose again, even so them also which sleep in Jesus will God bring with him. For this we say unto you by the word of the Lord, that we which are alive and remain unto the coming of the Lord shall not prevent them which are asleep. For the Lord himself shall descend from heaven with a shout, with the voice of the archangel, and with the trump of God: and the dead in Christ shall rise first: Then we which are alive and remain shall be caught up together with them in the clouds, to meet the Lord in the air: and so shall we ever be with the Lord. Wherefore comfort one another with these words."

You have received Jesus as Lord and Savior of your life and you are a child of Almighty God. You are God's children of the light. God has great things in store for the children of the kingdom. Jesus went away to prepare a place for us and He shall return. According to 1 Thessalonians 5:5-11, we read…

> *"Ye are all the children of light, and the children of the day: we are not of the night, nor of darkness. Therefore let us not sleep, as do others; but let us watch and be sober. For they that sleep sleep in the night; and they that be drunken are drunken in the night. But let us, who are of the day, be sober, putting on the breastplate of faith and love; and for an helmet, the hope of salvation. For God hath not appointed us to wrath, but to obtain salvation by our Lord Jesus Christ, Who died for us, that, whether we wake or sleep, we should live together with him. Wherefore comfort yourselves together, and edify one another, even as also ye do."*

REVELATION CHAPTER 21
SET FREE FROM THIS PRESENT EVIL WORLD
NEW HEAVEN AND A NEW EARTH

"And I saw a new heaven and a new earth: for the first heaven and the first earth were passed away; and there was no more sea. And I John saw the holy city, new Jerusalem, coming down from God out of heaven, prepared as a bride adorned for her husband. And I heard a great voice out of heaven saying, Behold, the tabernacle of God is with men, and he will dwell with them, and they shall be his people, and God himself shall be with them, and be their God. And God shall wipe away all tears from their eyes; and there shall be no more death, neither sorrow, nor crying, neither shall there be any more pain: for the former things are passed away. And he that sat upon the throne said, Behold, I make all things new. And he said unto me, Write: for these words are true and faithful. And he said unto me, It is done. I am Alpha and Omega, the beginning and the end. I will give unto him that is athirst of the fountain of the water of life freely. He that overcometh shall inherit all things; and I will be his God, and he shall be my son. But the fearful, and unbelieving, and the abominable, and murderers, and whoremongers, and sorcerers, and idolaters, and all liars, shall have their part in the lake which burneth with fire and brimstone: which is the second death. And there came unto me one of the seven angels which had the seven vials full of the seven last plagues, and talked with me, saying, Come hither, I will shew thee the bride, the Lamb's wife. And he carried me away in the spirit to a great and high mountain, and shewed me that great city, the holy Jerusalem, descending out of heaven from God, Having the glory of God: and her light was like unto a stone most precious, even like a jasper stone, clear as crystal; And had a wall great and high, and had twelve gates, and at the gates twelve angels, and names written thereon, which are the names of the twelve tribes of the children of Israel: On the east three gates; on the north three gates; on the south three gates; and on the west three gates. And the wall of the city had twelve foundations, and in them the names of the twelve apostles of the Lamb. And he that talked with me had a golden reed to measure the city, and the gates thereof, and the wall thereof. And the city lieth foursquare, and the length is as large as the breadth: and he measured the city with the reed, twelve thousand furlongs. The length and the

breadth and the height of it are equal. And he measured the wall thereof, an hundred and forty and four cubits, according to the measure of a man, that is, of the angel. And the building of the wall of it was of jasper: and the city was pure gold, like unto clear glass. And the foundations of the wall of the city were garnished with all manner of precious stones. The first foundation was jasper; the second, sapphire; the third, a chalcedony; the fourth, an emerald; The fifth, sardonyx; the sixth, sardius; the seventh, chrysolite; the eighth, beryl; the ninth, a topaz; the tenth, a chrysoprasus; the eleventh, a jacinth; the twelfth, an amethyst. And the twelve gates were twelve pearls; every several gate was of one pearl: and the street of the city was pure gold, as it were transparent glass. And I saw no temple therein: for the Lord God Almighty and the Lamb are the temple of it. And the city had no need of the sun, neither of the moon, to shine in it: for the glory of God did lighten it, and the Lamb is the light thereof. And the nations of them which are saved shall walk in the light of it: and the kings of the earth do bring their glory and honour into it. And the gates of it shall not be shut at all by day: for there shall be no night there. And they shall bring the glory and honour of the nations into it. And there shall in no wise enter into it any thing that defileth, neither whatsoever worketh abomination, or maketh a lie: but they which are written in the Lamb's book of life."

REVELATION CHAPTER 22
SURELY I COME QUICKLY

"And he shewed me a pure river of water of life, clear as crystal, proceeding out of the throne of God and of the Lamb. In the midst of the street of it, and on either side of the river, was there the tree of life, which bare twelve manner of fruits, and yielded her fruit every month: and the leaves of the tree were for the healing of the nations. And there shall be no more curse: but the throne of God and of the Lamb shall be in it; and his servants shall serve him: And they shall see his face; and his name shall be in their foreheads. And there shall be no night there; and they need no candle, neither light of the sun; for the Lord God giveth them light: and they shall reign for ever and ever. And he said unto me, These sayings are faithful and true: and the Lord God of the holy prophets sent his angel to shew unto his servants the things which must shortly be done. Behold, I come quickly: blessed is he that keepeth the sayings of the prophecy of this book. And I John saw these things, and heard them. And when I had heard and seen, I fell down to worship before the feet of the angel which shewed me these things. Then saith he unto me, See thou do it not: for I am thy fellowservant, and of thy brethren the prophets, and of them which keep the sayings of this book: worship God. And he saith unto me, Seal not the sayings of the prophecy of this book: for the time is at hand. He that is unjust, let him be unjust still: and he which is filthy, let him be filthy still: and he that is righteous, let him be righteous still: and he that is holy, let him be holy still. And, behold, I come quickly; and my reward is with me, to give every man according as his work shall be. I am Alpha and Omega, the beginning and the end, the first and the last. Blessed are they that do his commandments, that they may have right to the tree of life, and may enter in through the gates into the city. For without are dogs, and sorcerers, and whoremongers, and murderers, and idolaters, and whosoever loveth and maketh a lie. I Jesus have sent mine angel to testify unto you these things in the churches. I am the root and the offspring of David, and the bright and morning star. And the Spirit and the bride say, Come. And let him that heareth say, Come. And let him that is athirst come. And whosoever will, let him take the water of life freely. For I testify unto every man that heareth the words of the prophecy of this book, If any man shall add unto these things, God shall add unto him the plagues that are written in this book: And if any man shall take away from the words of the book of this prophecy, God shall take away his part out of the book of life, and out of the holy city, and from the things which are written in this book. He which testifieth these things saith, Surely I come quickly. Amen. Even so, come, Lord Jesus."

UNTIL THE LORD RETURNS WE MUST, JESUS SAID…

Luke 19:13
"OCCUPY TILL I COME"

REVELATION CHAPTER 12
THE KINGDOM OF OUR GOD

"THEY OVERCAME HIM BY THE BLOOD OF THE LAMB, AND BY THE WORD OF THEIR TESTIMONY…"

(Revelations 12:7-12)

"And there was war in heaven: Michael and his angels fought against the dragon; and the dragon fought and his angels, And prevailed not; neither was their place found any more in heaven. And the great dragon was cast out, that old serpent, called the Devil, and Satan, which deceiveth the whole world: he was cast out into the earth, and his angels were cast out with him. And I heard a loud voice saying in heaven, Now is come salvation, and strength, and the kingdom of our God, and the power of his Christ: for the accuser of our brethren is cast down, which accused them before our God day and night. And they overcame him by the blood of the Lamb, and by the word of their testimony; and they loved not their lives unto the death. Therefore rejoice, ye heavens, and ye that dwell in them. Woe to the inhabiters of the earth and of the sea! for the devil is come down unto you, having great wrath, because he knoweth that he hath but a short time."

REVELATION CHAPTER 20
THEY SHALL BE PRIESTS OF GOD
AND OF CHRIST

"And I saw an angel come down from heaven, having the key of the bottomless pit and a great chain in his hand. And he laid hold on the dragon, that old serpent, which is the Devil, and Satan, and bound him a thousand years, And cast him into the bottomless pit, and shut him up, and set a seal upon him, that he should deceive the nations no more, till the thousand years should be fulfilled: and after that he must be loosed a little season. And I saw thrones, and they sat upon them, and judgment was given unto them: and I saw the souls of them that were beheaded for the witness of Jesus, and for the word of God, and which had not worshipped the beast, neither his image, neither had received his mark upon their foreheads, or in their hands; and they lived and reigned with Christ a thousand years. But the rest of the dead lived not again until the thousand years were finished. This is the first resurrection. Blessed and holy is he that hath part in the first resurrection: on such the second death hath no power, but they shall be priests of God and of Christ, and shall reign with him a thousand years. And when the thousand years are expired, Satan shall be loosed out of his prison, And shall go out to deceive the nations which are in the four quarters of the earth, Gog and Magog, to gather them together to battle: the number of whom is as the sand of the sea. And they went up on the breadth of the earth, and compassed the camp of the saints about, and the beloved city: and fire came down from God out of heaven, and devoured them. And the devil that deceived them was cast into the lake of fire and brimstone, where the beast and the false prophet are, and shall be tormented day and night for ever and ever. And I saw a great white throne, and him that sat on it, from whose face the earth and the heaven fled away; and there was found no place for them. And I saw the dead, small and great, stand before God; and the books were opened: and another book was opened, which is the book of life: and the dead were judged out of those things which were written in the books, according to their works. And the sea gave up the dead which were in it; and death and hell delivered up the dead which were in them: and they were judged every man according to their works. And death and hell were cast into the lake of fire. This is the

second death. And whosoever was not found written in the book of life was cast into the lake of fire."

Revelation 21:1
"And I saw a new heaven and a new earth: for the first heaven and the first earth were passed away; and there was no more sea."

BUT THE DAY OF THE LORD WILL COME
THE LORD IS NOT SLACK
CONCERNING HIS PROMISE

2 Peter 3:8-18

"But, beloved, be not ignorant of this one thing, that one day is with the Lord as a thousand years, and a thousand years as one day. The Lord is not slack concerning his promise, as some men count slackness; but is longsuffering to us-ward, not willing that any should perish, but that all should come to repentance. But the day of the Lord will come as a thief in the night; in the which the heavens shall pass away with a great noise, and the elements shall melt with fervent heat, the earth also and the works that are therein shall be burned up. Seeing then that all these things shall be dissolved, what manner of persons ought ye to be in all holy conversation and godliness, Looking for and hasting unto the coming of the day of God, wherein the heavens being on fire shall be dissolved, and the elements shall melt with fervent heat? Nevertheless we, according to his promise, look for new heavens and a new earth, wherein dwelleth righteousness. Wherefore, beloved, seeing that ye look for such things, be diligent that ye may be found of him in peace, without spot, and blameless. And account that the longsuffering of our Lord is salvation; even as our beloved brother Paul also according to the wisdom given unto him hath written unto you; As also in all his epistles, speaking in them of these things; in which are some things hard to be understood, which they that are unlearned and unstable wrest, as they do also the other scriptures, unto their own destruction. Ye therefore, beloved, seeing ye know these things before, beware lest ye also, being led away with the error of the wicked, fall from your own stedfastness. But grow in grace, and in the knowledge of our Lord and Saviour Jesus Christ. To him be glory both now and for ever. Amen."

AN IN-DEPTH STUDY OF THE BOOK OF MATTHEW
(Chapters 1-10)

(PREPARE YE THE WAY OF THE LORD)

INTRODUCTION
PREPARE YE THE WAY OF THE LORD

Matthew 3:2
"And saying, Repent ye: for the kingdom of heaven is at hand."

Matthew 3:3
"For this is he that was spoken of by the prophet Esaias, saying, The voice of one crying in the wilderness, Prepare ye the way of the Lord, make his paths straight."

The prophets spoke of the kingdom of God, but it was long before their time. The natural kingdom was the Davidic Covenant Kingdom through his seed. (2 Samuel 7:7-16, 7:11, Psalms 89:3-4, Zechariah 12:8) College students and ministers, you will need to study the "Davidic Covenant" so that you can answer any questions your team members might have.

All other students, along with the new converts, your study will be centered on you becoming prepared for the Lord. Those who are prepared for the Lord are learning to live a Christian life looking unto Jesus as their example.

The New Testament is a New Covenant. The word "covenant" means "new agreement or new contract with better promises." In Hebrews 8:6 we read, "But now hath he obtained a more excellent ministry, by how much also he is the mediator of a better covenant, which was established upon better promises."

The "He" spoken of is God's only Son, Jesus Christ. The Old Testament spoke of death to the sinner. There were many laws that required the one who was seeking God that they had to do.

When the fullness of time came, "[16] God so loved the world, that he gave his only begotten Son, that whosoever believeth in him should not perish, but have everlasting life. [17] For God sent not his Son into the world to condemn the world; but that the world through him might be saved." (John 3:16-17)

After Jesus died on the cross as full payment for our past sins, present sins and future sins; He cried out on Calvary and said, "It is finished." It was no more what you had to do. Salvation comes by what Jesus did.

As you learn to live as a child of God, you serve Him and obey His Word because you love Him. After you have received Jesus as Savior and Lord of your life, ask God to fill you with the power of the Holy Ghost according to Acts.

Daily, you must prepare yourself for the wilderness and tribulations of the world through prayer and study of God's Word. Satan goes around as a roaring lion seeking whom he may devour. In Bible Study and church, you will learn to defeat the devil. You will say, "It is written."

UNTO CHRIST ARE FOURTEEN GENERATIONS

Matthew 1:17
"So all the generations from Abraham to David are fourteen generations; and from David until the carrying away into Babylon are fourteen generations; and from the carrying away into Babylon unto Christ are fourteen generations."

After Matthew completed what connected Jesus to His natural family through the linage of Joseph, Matthew quickly moved us into Jesus' true identity. Jesus Christ is the Son of God, Emmanuel, God with us.

Between the Old Testament and the New Testament there are approximately 400 years. These years are called silent years. Many theologians want us to think God was not at work. I strongly disagree with those 400 hundreds being silent years. I believe God was at work behind the scene preparing for the fullness of time. In Galatians 4:4-5 Paul writes [4] "But when the fulness of the time was come, God sent forth his Son, made of a woman, made under the law, [5] To redeem them that were under the law, that we might receive the adoption of sons."

The fullness of time came when God sent His only begotten Son, Jesus Christ, into the world born of a virgin by the Holy Ghost to die on cross as payment for the sins of the world. Everyone who confesses their sins, believe on the Lord Jesus Christ and receive Him as Savior of their life; they would be saved.

When you receive Jesus as Lord and Savior of your life, you were translated out of the kingdom of darkness into the kingdom of God's dear Son according to Colossians 1:13. Now that you have been translated out of the kingdom of darkness into the kingdom of God's dear Son, you need to know how to live like a child of the King.

In 1 Timothy 6:15 "Which in his times he shall shew, who is the blessed and only Potentate, the King of kings, and Lord of lords."

John wrote in Revelation 1:6 "And hath made us kings and priests unto God and his Father; to him be glory and dominion for ever and ever. Amen."

Also, Revelation 5:9-10 we read…

> "And they sung a new song, saying, Thou art worthy to take the book, and to open the seals thereof: for thou wast slain, and hast redeemed us to God by thy blood out of every kindred, and tongue, and people, and nation; And hast made us unto our God kings and priests: and we shall reign on the earth."

Through the gospel of Jesus Christ, you will learn how to live like a king. Through the power of Holy Spirit and your faith in the Word of God, you can live a victorious Christian life until Jesus, who is the King of kings and Lord of lords, return. It is written in Revelation 15:3, "And they sing the song of Moses the servant of God, and the song of the Lamb, saying, Great and marvellous are thy works, Lord God Almighty; just and true are thy ways, thou King of saints."

Until Jesus returns, we must get to know our King through the gospels of Jesus Christ. Then we can boldly decree as the Apostle decree in Romans 1:16, "For I am not ashamed of the gospel of Christ: for it is the power of God unto salvation to every one that believeth; to the Jew first, and also to the Greek." The gospel is not about power; it is the power of God unto salvation to everyone who believes.

As you begin every lesson with prayer, I believe through your knowledge of the Word of God, you will believe, receive, obey God's Word and receive your miracle. It does not matter if you are sick in your body; God has promised in Isaiah 53:4-5 which reads…

> Surely he hath borne our griefs, and carried our sorrows: yet we did esteem him stricken, smitten of God, and afflicted. But he was wounded for our transgressions, he was bruised for our iniquities: the chastisement of our peace was upon him; and with his stripes we are healed."

Evidence of Jesus' healing power is written in the gospels. There is evidence of Him supplying food for the hungry, water for the thirsty, money to pay overdue taxes and the raising of a woman's son to life. The miracles our King Jesus did yesterday is still being done today by us, His kings.

In Hebrews 13:8 we read, "Jesus Christ the same yesterday, and to day, and for ever." You might be wondering how these miracles are being performed today if Jesus is in heaven seated on the right hand of the Father making intercession for us. (Colossians 3:1). That is a great question and I can answer your question by the Word of God according to Hebrews 7:25 which read, "Wherefore he is able also to save them to the uttermost that come unto God by him, seeing he ever liveth to make intercession for them." Also, in Acts 1:2 we read, "Until the day in which he was taken up, after that he through the Holy Ghost had given commandments unto the apostles whom he had chosen."

The Spirit of God, which is the Holy Ghost, is at work in every Holy Ghost filled Christian. You are powerless without the infilling of the Holy Ghost. It is impossible for you to follow the example of Jesus without being full of the Holy Ghost. Jesus gave us a promise in Acts 1:8 which read, "But ye shall receive power, after that the Holy Ghost is come upon you: and ye shall be witnesses unto me both in Jerusalem, and in all Judaea, and in Samaria, and unto the uttermost part of the earth."
Every born again Christian, who has been filled with the Holy Ghost, received power over all power of the devil. Every Christian was given the measure of faith. (Romans 12:3). That measure will be added to and your faith will grow exceedingly until you believe you can do all things through Christ, who strengthens you. (Philippians 4:13).

The gospel of the kingdom is manifested in these last days. God is pouring His Spirit out upon all flesh and in Acts 2:17-21 we read…

"And it shall come to pass in the last days, saith God, I will pour out of my Spirit upon all flesh: and your sons and your daughters shall prophesy, and your young men shall see visions, and your old men shall dream dreams: And on my servants and on my handmaidens I will pour out in those days of my Spirit; and they shall prophesy:

And I will shew wonders in heaven above, and signs in the earth beneath; blood, and fire, and vapour of smoke: The sun shall be turned into darkness, and the moon into blood, before that great and notable day of the Lord come: And it shall come to pass, that whosoever shall call on the name of the Lord shall be saved."

The generation that is choosing to serve the King of kings and Lord of lords is the Jesus generation. They know their assignment. They realize they are a voice crying in the wilderness of a world of tribulation and trouble to prepare the way of the Lord.

There have been too many crooked places, but the Jesus generation has come on the scene with one motive to prepare the way of the Lord and make His path straight. Through the anointing and presence of God upon their lives, they will make ready a people prepared for the Lord. We are living in the last days and Jesus is soon to return. Ask yourself, "Have you been preparing the people for the Lord?" The whole creation is groaning for a manifestation of the sons of God. Romans 8:22 read, "For we know that the whole creation groaneth and travaileth in pain together until now."

When the true sons of God come in your presence, their heart is on preparing you for the Lord. They will become God's intercessors in your life and they will not be satisfied until they know you are being prepared for the Lord as you study to shew yourself approved unto God, a workman that need not to be ashamed, as you learn to rightly divide the Word of truth.

The study of God's Word is not an option. It is a command. You cannot know Him in the power of His resurrection and then be conformable unto His death without your knowledge of God's Word.

It is God's perfect will that you know Him and for you to be prepared for the Lord. The only way you can be prepared for the Lord is through the power of Holy Spirit and the Word of God.

The Word of God, through the power of the Holy Ghost, will prepare you for the Lord. When you are prepared for the Lord in your prayer, praise, worship and the preaching and teaching of God's Word, the Lord whom you seek shall suddenly come to His temple. Malachi 3:1 read, "Behold, I will send my messenger, and he shall prepare the way before me: and the Lord, whom ye seek, shall suddenly come to this temple, even the messenger of the covenant, whom ye delight in: behold, he shall come, saith the LORD of hosts."

As you study the gospel of Matthew (Part 1), allow Holy Spirit to lead and guide you into all truths. Prepare yourself for the Lord and expect God to bring restoration to every area of your life as you become transformed into the image of God's dear Son. The sons of God will rule and reign as children of the King. The gospel of Matthew begins with Jesus' birth which took place about 5-4 B.C. and began His ministry at age 30. Jesus taught and preached for three years. In those three years, Jesus was a demonstration and manifestation of the power of God and the kingdom of heaven.

John the Baptist prepared the way for Jesus. He was a voice crying in the wilderness. Jesus came into the world, ministered for three years, crucified, buried, rose from the dead and went back to heaven. During Jesus' three years of ministry, Jesus spent quality time into His disciples making them and preparing them for God.

Written in the gospels are the principles Jesus used to make and prepare His disciples for God. Jesus knew He would soon return back to the Father. After His departure, the disciples must do what Jesus had taught them to do and also make and prepare a people for Jesus.

This time of preparation began in the lives of the apostles after they were filled with the Holy Ghost. They went throughout the (then known world) preaching and teaching Christ. Christ confirmed their message with signs and miracles following.

As you study the gospel of Matthew, I pray God will allow Holy Spirit to lead and guide us into all truths. We are living in the last days, a day when Jesus is pouring out His Spirit upon all flesh. The people of God is being prepared and made ready for the Lord, the gospel of Matthew and the Word of God. Are you ready to be prepared and made ready for the Lord?

Matthew's name mean "gift of Jehovah." He was a tax collector until he met Jesus. After he met Jesus, he became a disciple and a follower of Christ. He was a witness of Jesus' ministry and he wrote the things he had seen and heard.

The approximate date was around A.D. 58-68. There are 15 parables and 20 miracles in Matthew. Matthew lists 10 parables and 3 miracles that you will not find in the other 3 gospels.

In Matthew 27:51-52, we read of the saints who came out of the grave after Jesus rose from the dead. Only Matthew recorded this miracle. Truly, this is the Son of God prophesied in the Old Testament that was coming into the world. Emmanuel (God with us) had come; redemption took place.

MATTHEW CHAPTER ONE

JESUS' EARTHLY AND SPIRITUAL GENERATION
EMMANUEL - GOD WITH US

Matthew 1:1-17

"The book of the generation of Jesus Christ, the son of David, the son of Abraham. Abraham begat Isaac; and Isaac begat Jacob; and Jacob begat Judas and his brethren; And Judas begat Phares and Zara of Thamar; and Phares begat Esrom; and Esrom begat Aram; And Aram begat Aminadab; and Aminadab begat Naasson; and Naasson begat Salmon; And Salmon begat Booz of Rachab; and Booz begat Obed of Ruth; and Obed begat Jesse; And Jesse begat David the king; and David the king begat Solomon of her that had been the wife of Urias; And Solomon begat Roboam; and Roboam begat Abia; and Abia begat Asa; And Asa begat Josaphat; and Josaphat begat Joram; and Joram begat Ozias; And Ozias begat Joatham; and Joatham begat Achaz; and Achaz begat Ezekias; And Ezekias begat Manasses; and Manasses begat Amon; and Amon begat Josias; And Josias begat Jechonias and his brethren, about the time they were carried away to Babylon: And after they were brought to Babylon, Jechonias begat Salathiel; and Salathiel begat Zorobabel; And Zorobabel begat Abiud; and Abiud begat Eliakim; and Eliakim begat Azor; And Azor begat Sadoc; and Sadoc begat Achim; and Achim begat Eliud; And Eliud begat Eleazar; and Eleazar begat Matthan; and Matthan begat Jacob; And Jacob begat Joseph the husband of Mary, of whom was born Jesus, who is called Christ. So all the generations from Abraham to David are fourteen generations; and from David until the carrying away into Babylon are fourteen generations; and from the carrying away into Babylon unto Christ are fourteen generations."

The genealogies of Jesus are traced through His adopted father, Joseph. (Luke 4:22). That was Jesus' natural family line. The genealogy through His adopted parents, Mary and Joseph. In Jesus' natural genealogy, there was Rahab the harlot; David the adulterer and murderer and many other relatives with a marred past.

This lets us know that it does not matter about your past; what matters is that God is with you. To have a new beginning, you must choose to be with God. No one can make that choice for you. You can remain a prisoner of your past or you can choose to be with God and He will become your heavenly Father. When you choose to be with God, you will need to know your heavenly Father. God has allowed holy men of God to write about Him and His Son Jesus in the Bible. As you study God's Word, your mind will be renewed, your faith will grow and you will get to know God and obey His Word.

GOD IS WITH US

Matthew 1:22-23

"Now all this was done, that it might be fulfilled which was spoken of the Lord by the prophet, saying, Behold, a virgin shall be with child, and shall bring forth a son, and they shall call his name Emmanuel, which being interpreted is, God with us."

Matthew 1:18-24

"Now the birth of Jesus Christ was on this wise: When as his mother Mary was espoused to Joseph, before they came together, she was found with child of the Holy Ghost. Then Joseph her husband, being a just man, and not willing to make her a publick example, was minded to put her away privily. But while he thought on these things, behold, the angel of the Lord appeared unto him in a dream, saying, Joseph, thou son of David, fear not to take unto thee Mary thy wife: for that which is conceived in her is of the Holy Ghost.

The First Old Testament Prophesy Being Fulfilled

Matthew 1:21-24

And she shall bring forth a son, and thou shalt call his name JESUS: for he shall save his people from their sins. Now all this was done, that it might be fulfilled which was spoken of the Lord by the prophet, saying, Behold, a virgin shall be with child, and shall bring forth a son, and they shall call his name Emmanuel, which being interpreted is, God with us. Then Joseph being raised from sleep did as the angel of the Lord had bidden him, and took unto him his wife:"

Jesus is not about the kingdom of God and the kingdom of heaven. He is the King and He possesses the kingdom. In Isaiah 9:2-7 we read…

"The people that walked in darkness have seen a great light: they that dwell in the land of the shadow of death, upon them hath the light shined. Thou hast multiplied the nation, and not increased the joy: they joy before thee according to the joy in harvest, and as men rejoice when they divide the spoil. For thou hast broken the yoke of his burden, and the staff of his shoulder, the rod of his oppressor, as in the day of Midian. For every battle of the warrior is with confused noise, and garments rolled in blood; but this shall be with burning and fuel of fire. For unto us a child is born, unto us a son is given: and the government shall be upon his shoulder: and his name shall be called Wonderful, Counseller, The mighty God, The everlasting Father, The Prince of Peace. Of the increase of his government and peace there shall be no end, upon the throne of David, and upon his kingdom, to order it, and to establish it with judgment and with justice from henceforth even for ever. The zeal of the LORD of hosts will perform this."

Jesus is truly the King of kings. He came to receive us into Himself, fill us with His Spirit and teach us to live and act like children of the Most High God. We are children of King Jesus.

When God is with you, you can expect God to call you out of the place where you are to bring you into a place where you can fulfill His divine purpose for your life. In Genesis 12:1-9, God called Abraham out of his father's country. This is a type of the world, sin and the kingdom of darkness.

God told Abraham His plan and purpose was to be with him and make him a great nation. Abraham and Sarah were old. They were passed the child bearing age. It did not matter about the natural man, which deals with the first nature, which is the Adam nature. All of us have the second nature. That second nature is our God nature.

In 1 Corinthians 15:45-49 Paul writes…

> *"And so it is written, The first man Adam was made a living soul; the last Adam was made a quickening spirit. Howbeit that was not first which is spiritual, but that which is natural; and afterward that which is spiritual. The first man is of the earth, earthy: the second man is the Lord from heaven. As is the earthy, such are they also that are earthy: and as is the heavenly, such are they also that are heavenly. And as we have borne the image of the earthy, we shall also bear the image of the heavenly."*

Abraham and Sarah's natural genealogy produced a body that could not bring forth in the natural. God was with Abraham and Sarah. God called them out of a pagan notation of sin and death. The day Abraham and Sarah chose to be with God, God began to reverse their body of death so that it could produce life.

There is always a process before there is an impartation and revelation of God's promise. During the process, you must remember the promises of God. "For all the promises of God are yea and in Him amen." (2 Corinthians 1:20). When it looks as if a promise is not coming to pass, you must ask yourself, "Am I with God?" To be with God is to be in agreement with His Word.

If you have been praying about a love one and it looks as if your prayers are not being answered, ask yourself are they with God. There is power in agreement. God loved the world so much until God is with every soul in the world giving them the breath of life.

The breath of life will not get you into heaven. The only way you can get into heaven is by you accepting Jesus Christ (who is eternal life) into your heart. Through Jesus Christ you receive life eternal and you are with God. With God all things are possible.

Every day you must "Choose ye this day whom you will serve." God is with you, but are you with God?

When Abraham and Sarah made a choice to be with God, the process began. In the midst of the process, they faced many problems. These problems helped their faith to grow exceedingly.
Ten years later, they received the promise. Never forget, there will be a process and there will be problems; but God always keep His promises.

MATTHEW CHAPTER ONE
DISCIPLESHIP, LEADERSHIP, MINISTRY & BIBLE COLLEGE STUDY QUESTIONS

History tells us the gospel of Matthew was written about 58-68 A.D. for the Jewish audience who had been waiting for their long awaiting King of Israel. The long awaited King over the kingdom of God. I praise God for inviting the world to share in the good news of the King and His kingdom.

The gospel of Jesus Christ is that the King has translated us out of the kingdom of darkness into the kingdom of His dear Son. Now, we must learn to live as children of the kingdom.

1. What is the process of Salvation? (Please use scripture)

_____
_____
_____

2. How many souls have you led to our Lord Jesus Christ this year?

_____

3. How many souls were filled with the Holy Ghost according to Acts 2:38? _____

4. What was Jesus' mission and His ministry according to Matthew chapter one?_____

_____
_____

5. Define "Jesus" according to Scripture _____

_____
_____
_____

The Apostle Paul said in Philippians 3:10 "That I may know him, and the power of his resurrection, and the fellowship of his sufferings, being made conformable unto his death."

Now it is time for the body of Christ to know Him. I believe as we embrace the Word of God and allow Holy Spirit to lead and guide us into all truths; we will never be the same. God's desire is to reveal Himself to us in these last days.

6. What has God showed you about Himself or His Son in chapter one of Matthew?

_____
_____
_____

Don't forget there has to be two or three witnesses. God spoke to you, now allow the Word of God to agree with you. The Word of God is the sure word of prophecy.

MATTHEW CHAPTER ONE
YOUTH & TEEN STUDY QUESTIONS

Name_____ Date_____ Grade_____

1. You will be studying the gospel of Matthew. Do you know what the word "gospel" mean?_____
(That word "gospel" means "Good News.")

2. Have you heard any bad news lately?_____

3. If your answer is "yes" will you briefly tell us the worse news you have heard lately. _____
_____
_____

4. How did you feel when you heard the bad news? _____
_____
_____

Note! There was bad news all over, the then known world, when Jesus was born. God saw all of the hurting people in the world and the bad news they were hearing. John 3:16-17 tells us what God did about the hurting people in the world. It reads…

> "For God so loved the world, that he gave his only begotten Son, that whosoever believeth in him should not perish, but have everlasting life. For God sent not his Son into the world to condemn the world; but that the world through him might be saved."

5. Your homework is to learn these two verses. As you meditate on these verses to learn them, God will heal your hurts.

You learned the verses –

John 3:16_____ Date_____

John 3:17_____ Date_____

MATTHEW CHAPTER TWO
WISE MEN COME TO WORSHIP JESUS

Matthew 2:1-4

"Now when Jesus was born in Bethlehem of Judaea in the days of Herod the king, behold, there came wise men from the east to Jerusalem, Saying, Where is he that is born King of the Jews? for we have seen his star in the east, and are come to worship him. When Herod the king had heard these things, he was troubled, and all Jerusalem with him. And when he had gathered all the chief priests and scribes of the people together, he demanded of them where Christ should be born."

The gathering of the chief priests and Scribes was to receive information of the place of Jesus' birth. The Scribes were not only writers of the law, but they were also teachers of the law. They knew of the Old Testament prophecies of Christ coming into the world. They also knew He was the King and the government would be upon His shoulders and of His kingdom there would be no end.

Herod heard the news of a New King of the Jews. He thought this King was going to take his earthly throne from him. His motive was not to find out where Jesus was born so he could worship Him; but his plot was to kill Jesus.

Old Testament prophecy is now being fulfilled through Jesus. God always keep His promises. The first fulfillment of prophecy is Matthew 1:22-23 which reads…

"Now all this was done, that it might be fulfilled which was spoken of the Lord by the prophet, saying, Behold, a virgin shall be with child, and shall bring forth a son, and they shall call his name Emmanuel, which being interpreted is, God with us."

The Second Old Testament Prophecy Being Fulfilled

Matthew 2:5-14

"And they said unto him, In Bethlehem of Judaea: for thus it is written by the prophet, And thou Bethlehem, in the land of Juda, art not the least among the princes of Juda: for out of thee shall come a Governor, that shall rule my people Israel. Then Herod, when he had privily called the wise men, inquired of them diligently what time the star appeared. And he sent them to Bethlehem, and said, Go and search diligently for the young child; and when ye have found him, bring me word again, that I may come and worship him also. When they had heard the king, they departed; and, lo, the star, which they saw in the east, went before them, till it came and stood over where the young child was. When they saw the star, they rejoiced with exceeding great joy. And when they were come into the house, they saw the young child with Mary his mother, and fell down, and worshipped him: and when they had opened their treasures, they presented unto him gifts; gold, and frankincense, and myrrh. And being warned of God in a dream that they should not return to Herod, they departed into their own country another way. And when they were departed, behold, the angel of the Lord appeareth to Joseph in a dream, saying, Arise, and take the young child and his mother, and flee into Egypt, and be thou there until I bring thee word: for Herod will seek the young child to destroy him. When he arose, he took the young child and his mother by night, and departed into Egypt:"

Micah prophesied of Jesus' birth and His rejection in Micah 5:2 which reads, "But thou, Bethlehem Ephratah, though thou be little among the thousands of Judah, yet out of thee shall he come forth unto me that is to be ruler in Israel; whose goings forth have been from of old, from everlasting." Take special note, that focus of our attention should be on the young child and not on Mary, his mother. If you would take note in verse 11, they saw the young child with Mary, His mother. Our attention should always be on Jesus.

The wise men did not bow down and worship Mary. They fell down and worshipped Jesus. Your spirit, soul and body should be worshipping Jesus when you enter into the place where He has been birthed. You will only find Him birthed in the place where there is a falling down to worship Jesus.

In verse 11b it reads, "…and fell down, and worshipped him…" Pride cannot dwell in His presence. To fall down is to humble yourself in the presence of God. It takes a sacrifice of self. Before they presented their gifts, they presented themselves in worship.

After they had fallen down in worship to Jesus, the presented their gifts of…
- Gold – a symbol of deity
- Frankincense – The purity of our Lord Jesus Christ's life and the fragrance it would leave every place Jesus went while here on earth.
- Myrrh – The myrrh is a spice used in burials. It speaks of Jesus' suffering for the sins of the world. He would suffer and die on the cross as payment for the sins of the world.

Those gifts testified of what Jesus was going to do for us. When Jesus returns again, He will be presented gifts again. These gifts will not represent pain and sorrow. In Isaiah 60:6 we read, "The multitude of camels shall cover thee, the dromedaries of Midian and Ephah; all they from Sheba shall come: they shall bring gold and incense; and they shall shew forth the praises of the LORD."

He will only be presented gold and incense. Did you notice, myrrh will not be presented to Him? When Jesus suffered and died on the cross, that was once and it was for all.

The Third Old Testament Prophecy Being Fulfilled

Matthew 2:15-16

"And was there until the death of Herod: that it might be fulfilled which was spoken of the Lord by the prophet, saying, Out of Egypt have I called my son. Then Herod, when he saw that he was mocked of the wise men, was exceeding wroth, and sent forth, and slew all the children that were in Bethlehem, and in all the coasts thereof, from two years old and under, according to the time which he had diligently inquired of the wise men."

Hosea was the first minor prophet. He prophesied these words in Hosea 11:1 between 770-725 B.C. which reads, "When Israel was a child, then I loved him, and called my son out of Egypt." God called His Son Jesus out of Israel. Every prophecy agrees with the plan of God.

The Fourth Old Testament Prophecy Being Fulfilled

Matthew 2:17-22

"Then was fulfilled that which was spoken by Jeremy the prophet, saying, In Rama was there a voice heard, lamentation, and weeping, and great mourning, Rachel weeping for her children, and would not be comforted, because they are not. But when Herod was dead, behold, an angel of the Lord appeareth in a dream to Joseph in Egypt, Saying, Arise, and take the young child and his mother, and go into the land of Israel: for they are dead which sought the young child's life. And he arose, and took the young child and his mother, and came into the land of Israel. But when he heard that Archelaus did reign in Judaea in the room of his father Herod, he was afraid to go thither: notwithstanding, being warned of God in a dream, he turned aside into the parts of Galilee:"

The prophet Jeremiah prophesied of the weeping in Jeremiah 31:15 which read, "Thus saith the LORD; A voice was heard in Ramah, lamentation, and bitter weeping; Rahel weeping for her children refused to be comforted for her children, because they were not."

The Fifth Old Testament Prophecy is also Fulfilled

Matthew 2:23

"And he came and dwelt in a city called Nazareth: that it might be fulfilled which was spoken by the prophets, He shall be called a Nazarene."

In Isaiah 11:1-2 the prophet writes…

"And there shall come forth a rod out of the stem of Jesse, and a Branch shall grow out of his roots: And the spirit of the LORD shall rest upon him, the spirit of wisdom and understanding, the spirit of counsel and might, the spirit of knowledge and of the fear of the LORD"

MATTHEW CHAPTER TWO
YOUTH & TEEN STUDY QUESTIONS

Name_____ Date_____ Grade_____

1. Where was Jesus born? _____

2. Who was the King? _____

3. Who was Jesus to be King over? _____

4. What did King Herod do when he heard King Jesus was going to be born? _____
_____
_____

5. When the wise men found Jesus what did they do?
_____
_____
_____

6. What is worship? _____
_____
_____

7. How did the wise men find Jesus? _____
_____

Name the three gifts they gave Jesus:
8. _____

9. _____

10. _____

What did you learn from this lesson that you can apply to your life and help you grow in your faith as a Christian?

_____
_____
_____
_____
_____
_____
_____
_____
_____

MATTHEW CHAPTER TWO
DISCIPLESHIP, LEADERSHIP, MINISTRY & BIBLE COLLEGE STUDY QUESTIONS

1. Did you read your chapter and complete your summary of chapter two? _____

_____

2. Did Holy Spirit reveal to you present truths concerning this lesson?

_____

If your answer is "yes" please write down God's present truths. Always keep in mind, present truths will always agree with the Word of God. That's what the fulfillment of prophecy is all about.

_____

_____

_____

_____

3. Define the process of worship according to the lesson.

_____

_____

According to this lesson define the following:

4. Gold - _____

5. Frankincense - _____

6. Myrrh - _____

7. How many Old Testament prophecies were fulfilled in chapters 1 & 2?_____

8. What was the third fulfillment of prophecy? _____

_____

9. The fourth fulfillment of prophecy?_____
_____
_____

10. Who was weeping for her children?_____

MATTHEW CHAPTER THREE
PREPARE YE THE WAY OF THE LORD

Matthew 3:1

"In those days came John the Baptist, preaching in the wilderness of Judaea."

The Six Old Testament Prophecy Being Fulfilled

In this prophecy God promised David his seed would rule over a kingdom that would have no end. It is called the Davidic Covenant. In 2 Samuel 7:7-13, it reads…

> *"In all the places wherein I have walked with all the children of Israel spake I a word with any of the tribes of Israel, whom I commanded to feed my people Israel, saying, Why build ye not me an house of cedar? Now therefore so shalt thou say unto my servant David, Thus saith the LORD of hosts, I took thee from the sheepcote, from following the sheep, to be ruler over my people, over Israel: And I was with thee whithersoever thou wentest, and have cut off all thine enemies out of thy sight, and have made thee a great name, like unto the name of the great men that are in the earth. Moreover I will appoint a place for my people Israel, and will plant them, that they may dwell in a place of their own, and move no more; neither shall the children of wickedness afflict them any more, as beforetime, And as since the time that I commanded judges to be over my people Israel, and have caused thee to rest from all thine enemies. Also the LORD telleth thee that he will make thee an house. And when thy days be fulfilled, and thou shalt sleep with thy fathers, I will set up thy seed after thee, which shall proceed out of thy bowels, and I will establish his kingdom. He shall build an house for my name, and I will stablish the throne of his kingdom for ever."*

The kingdom of God is an everlasting kingdom. In Daniel 4:2-3, we read…

> *"I thought it good to shew the signs and wonders that the high God*

hath wrought toward me. How great are his signs! and how mighty are his wonders! his kingdom is an everlasting kingdom, and his dominion is from generation to generation."

Jesus, The King, was present among the people. He dwelled among them to establish the kingdom. The kingdom began when Jesus came into the earth and His kingdom will continue on throughout all eternity.

Jesus Christ is what the kingdom of God and the kingdom of heaven is all about. In Romans 14:17-18, we read…

"For the kingdom of God is not meat and drink; but righteousness, and peace, and joy in the Holy Ghost. For he that in these things serveth Christ is acceptable to God, and approved of men."

That is kingdom living. Kingdom living takes place in you when you allow King Jesus to rule and reign in and through your life. Luke wrote in Luke 17:20-21…

"And when he was demanded of the Pharisees, when the kingdom of God should come, he answered them and said, The kingdom of God cometh not with observation: Neither shall they say, Lo here! or, lo there! for, behold, the kingdom of God is within you."

When you received Jesus as Savior and Lord of your life, you received the kingdom of God. The day will come when we are either caught up in the rapture when Jesus comes on a cloud or we will be carried up when we are absent from this body in death and present with the Lord. We will end up in the kingdom of heaven.

Until that day come, we must occupy until He come and be a manifestation of the kingdom of God.

JOHN THE BAPTIST MINISTRY

Matthew 3:1

"In those days came John the Baptist, preaching in the wilderness of Judaea."

The wilderness of Judaea was a barren wasteland. When you have been prepared by God to do the work of His ministry, even the barren wasteland will become a fruitful place for souls.

It does not matter if there is only one soul a month translated out of the kingdom of darkness into the kingdom of God's dear Son; you have been called, anointed and appointed by God into ministry. The word of God confirms the proof of your ministry by your evangelistic work. Every born-again Christian is to be a soul winner. In 2 Timothy 4:5 we read, "But watch thou in all things, endure afflictions, do the work of an evangelist, make full proof of thy ministry."

Every Spirit-filled Christian young and old, once they have received Jesus and living a kingdom life of righteousness, joy and peace in the Holy Ghost; you should tell others about this kingdom life. John knew the kingdom of God message begin with "repentance." John cried out in Matthew 3:2, "And saying, Repent ye: for the kingdom of heaven is at hand."

To be "at hand" means, "God's presence is in your midst." When the presence of God is upon His men and women of God, the kingdom of God is in your midst. (Repent – means to change your mind.)

God allowed Isaiah to have a revelation of the future when John the Baptist would be the fulfillment of this prophecy. In Isaiah 40:3 it reads, "The voice of him that crieth in the wilderness, Prepare ye the way of the LORD, make straight in the desert a highway for our God."

We have been called by God to "prepare the way of the Lord." "To prepare" is to furnish and equip for the presence of the Lord. When you pray, praise and worship Jesus, you are being furnished by God.

75

As the men and women of God, whom God has appointed to preach and teach His Word; you shall become equip to bring the lost to Jesus.

The desert place might be your family you have been trying to bring into the kingdom of God, but they will not leave their dry place of sin. It might by your place of employment, your neighborhood or spouse. Always remember, no desert is so dry that the presence and power of God cannot water. God will water the dry places as you continue to tell them about Jesus. It is God who will cause them to see the kingdom of God. In John 3:1-3, Jesus tells Nicodemus how to see the kingdom of God. It reads…

> *"There was a man of the Pharisees, named Nicodemus, a ruler of the Jews: The same came to Jesus by night, and said unto him, Rabbi, we know that thou art a teacher come from God: for no man can do these miracles that thou doest, except God be with him. Jesus answered and said unto him, Verily, verily, I say unto thee, Except a man be born again, he cannot see the kingdom of God."*

When you are born-again, you are born into the kingdom of God. You have a change of mind and a change of heart. John the Baptist's sermon, To Prepare the People for the Lord and to Make His Paths Straight, continued on through Matthew 3:4-12 which reads…

> *"And the same John had his raiment of camel's hair, and a leathern girdle about his loins; and his meat was locusts and wild honey. Then went out to him Jerusalem, and all Judaea, and all the region round about Jordan, And were baptized of him in Jordan, confessing their sins. But when he saw many of the Pharisees and Sadducees come to his baptism, he said unto them, O generation of vipers, who hath warned you to flee from the wrath to come? Bring forth therefore fruits meet for repentance: And think not to say within yourselves, We have Abraham to our father: for I say unto you, that God is able of these stones to raise up children unto Abraham. And now also the axe is laid unto the root of the trees: therefore every tree which bringeth not forth good fruit is hewn down, and cast into the fire. I indeed baptize you with water unto repentance: but he that cometh after me is mightier than I, whose shoes I am not worthy to bear: he shall baptize you with the Holy Ghost, and with fire: Whose fan is in his hand, and he will throughly*

purge his floor, and gather his wheat into the garner; but he will burn up the chaff with unquenchable fire."

You are new converts. Do not mistake John the Baptist with John the Revelator. John the Baptist was Jesus' cousin. After he had completed his ministry, he was arrested and later beheaded for the gospel of Jesus Christ. John the Revelator wrote the book of Revelation, which we are looking forward to studying if the Lord delays His coming.

John the Baptist's message contains a three-fold message of the gospel of Jesus Christ and His kingdom. He begins preaching the message of repentance. Then John moves quickly into the baptism in water. There is a brief pause, and then John the Baptist reveals who the baptizer is with these words…

Matthew 3:11

"…but he that cometh after me is mightier than I, whose shoes I am not worthy to bear: he shall baptize you with the Holy Ghost, and with fire."

Jesus is the baptizer. For many years, the church thought if they fast long enough and prayed intensely calling on the name of Jesus; the people would receive the Holy Ghost.

We are not in charge of the Holy Ghost. All these things are good, but we should not try to bargain with God. You should pray because you enjoy communion and fellowship with God. Praise and worship should be a part of every believer's life. Praise is truly what we do in the midst of our troubles and tribulations.

It is in the midst of our prayers, praise, worship and God's Word that Jesus come and baptize believers in the Holy Ghost. The baptism in the Holy Ghost does not only take place in the house of God, but God will baptize any place and any time Jesus Christ chooses. If you are not sure you have been filled with the Holy Ghost according to Acts 2:1-4, ask Jesus to fill you with the Holy Ghost this very hour.

JESUS CHRIST IS BAPTIZED

Matthew 3:13-17

"Then cometh Jesus from Galilee to Jordan unto John, to be baptized of him. But John forbad him, saying, I have need to be baptized of thee, and comest thou to me? And Jesus answering said unto him, Suffer it to be so now: for thus it becometh us to fulfil all righteousness. Then he suffered him. And Jesus, when he was baptized, went up straightway out of the water: and, lo, the heavens were opened unto him, and he saw the Spirit of God descending like a dove, and lighting upon him: And lo a voice from heaven, saying, This is my beloved Son, in whom I am well pleased."

Jesus received His identification from God, the Father. It is not that Jesus did not know who He was; His identification came from God so that the world would know. With Jesus' identification came an impartation. When we speak of an impartation, God gives you the measure of faith so that you will be able to withstand every attack of the devil.

In chapter four, you will find Jesus being led up by Holy Spirit into the wilderness to be tempted or tested by the devil. The wilderness is a type of the world. You have power through the Holy Ghost, the blood of Jesus and the Word of God. "And they overcame him by the blood of the Lamb, and by the word of their testimony; and they loved not their lives unto the death." (Revelation 12:11)

MATTHEW CHAPTER THREE
YOUTH & TEEN STUDY QUESTIONS

Name_____ Date_____ Grade_____

1. Who was preaching in the wilderness? _____

2. Why do you think God told him to preach in the wilderness? (The wilderness of John's day is like the evil and sin in the world today.)
_____
_____

3. Read John 3:16-17... Why did God send His only Son, Jesus, into the world? _____
_____

4. What is "Salvation?" _____
_____

5. Who needs to be saved? _____
_____

6. What is "Sin?" _____
_____

7. What is "Baptism?" _____
_____

8. Why do you need to be baptized? _____
_____

9. Are you God's Son?_____ (John 1:12)

10. What can you apply to your life from this chapter?
_____
_____
_____

MATTHEW CHAPTER THREE
DISCIPLESHIP, LEADERSHIP, MINISTRY
& BIBLE COLLEGE STUDY QUESTIONS

1. Did you complete your summaries of chapter three? _____

2. Where was John the Baptist called to minister?_____
_____

3. John had three messages, name and define them with Scripture.
(1)_____
(2)_____
(3)_____

4. John mentions two baptisms, name and define them with Scripture.
(1)_____
(2)_____

5. Briefly define verse 12. _____
_____

6. Why was Jesus baptized? _____
_____

7. Three things took place when Jesus was baptized, what were they?
(1)_____
(2)_____
(3)_____

8. Was John related to Jesus? _____

9. If your answer is "yes" how were they related? _____
_____

10. What did you learn from this chapter that you can apply to your
daily life? _____
_____

MATTHEW CHAPTER FOUR
THE LORD JESUS CHRIST TEMPTED
BY THE DEVIL

Matthew 4:1-11

"Then was Jesus led up of the Spirit into the wilderness to be tempted of the devil. And when he had fasted forty days and forty nights, he was afterward an hungred. And when the tempter came to him, he said, If thou be the Son of God, command that these stones be made bread. But he answered and said, It is written, Man shall not live by bread alone, but by every word that proceedeth out of the mouth of God. Then the devil taketh him up into the holy city, and setteth him on a pinnacle of the temple, And saith unto him, If thou be the Son of God, cast thyself down: for it is written, He shall give his angels charge concerning thee: and in their hands they shall bear thee up, lest at any time thou dash thy foot against a stone. Jesus said unto him, It is written again, Thou shalt not tempt the Lord thy God. Again, the devil taketh him up into an exceeding high mountain, and sheweth him all the kingdoms of the world, and the glory of them; And saith unto him, All these things will I give thee, if thou wilt fall down and worship me. Then saith Jesus unto him, Get thee hence, Satan: for it is written, Thou shalt worship the Lord thy God, and him only shalt thou serve. Then the devil leaveth him, and, behold, angels came and ministered unto him."

Jesus was not led down to be tempted by the devil; he was led up. He was led into the place where principalities, powers and spiritual wickedness in high places dwell. In Ephesians 6:12 we read, "For we wrestle not against flesh and blood, but against principalities, against powers, against the rulers of the darkness of this world, against spiritual wickedness in high places."

Jesus went into the wilderness being led by the Holy Ghost to be tempted or tested by the devil. Jesus knew God was with Him and He knew He was going to have power over every attack of the devil. Jesus went before us and conquered every attack of the devil that we would one day face. We must boldly decree 2 Corinthians 2:14 which read, "Now thanks be unto God, which always causeth us to triumph in Christ, and maketh manifest the savour of his knowledge by us in every place."

The first area of Jesus' life Satan came to tempt Him in was His desire for food. Any desire to satisfy the flesh can only be conquered by the Word of God. You must know what is written.

When you eat natural food, your flesh will become fat. When you eat spiritual food (which is the Word of God you study and choose to obey), you will grow in the Spirit. You will grow in grace (this grace is God's enabling power) and in the knowledge of our Lord and Savior Jesus Christ.

Jesus spoke to the devil and said in Matthew 4:4, "…It is written, Man shall not live by bread alone, but by every word that proceedeth out of the mouth of God." These words were also spoken in Deuteronomy 8:3.

In Matthew 4:3-10, Jesus reveals every area of your life the devil will come to tempt you. Jesus also reveals His power to overcome the devil in area of His life. This same power has been given to every Spirit-filled Christian young and old. In Acts 1:8 Jesus said, "But ye shall receive power, after that the Holy Ghost is come upon you: and ye shall be witnesses unto me both in Jerusalem, and in all Judaea, and in Samaria, and unto the uttermost part of the earth."

You will know you have been filled with the Holy Ghost when you…

1. Speak with other tongues (Acts 2:4)
2. You receive power to live for Jesus
3. You witness about Jesus dying on the cross, giving His life as payment for the sins of the world. Jesus rose on the third day, went back to heaven and will return on a cloud to catch all Christians up. (Acts 1:8-11; 1 Thessalonians 4:11-18). While tribulation is going on, on the earth, all Christians young and old will be at the Marriage Supper of the Lamb. To help you understand what you have read, read the following Scriptures – (Revelation 19:1-10).

It is the will of God that every man, woman, boy and girl be saved. Every time we gather in a church service or Bible Study, the invitation should be given to those who have not received Jesus as Lord and Savior of their lives and also for those who desire to rededicate their life to Jesus. You cannot enter into the kingdom of heaven without Jesus.

Jesus defeated the devil in every area so that every Christian would be able to defeat the devil when he tries to tempt them to sin. Take a brief look at the areas Jesus defeated the devil. Jesus did not fight with weapons of this world, but He fought with the Word of God. The Word of God coming out of the mouth of a Holy Ghost filled Christian will defeat the devil every time. You must have faith in God and believe 2 Corinthians 10:4-5 which read…

> *("For the weapons of our warfare are not carnal, but mighty through God to the pulling down of strong holds;) Casting down imaginations, and every high thing that exalteth itself against the knowledge of God, and bringing into captivity every thought to the obedience of Christ."*

1. The tempter came first to test Jesus when He was hungry, to satisfy His flesh by turning stones to bread. It wasn't that Satan was concern with Jesus' hunger; he just wanted Jesus to lose sight of the power of God's Word. Jesus spoke to him and said, "…It is written, Man shall not live by bread alone, but by every word that proceedeth out of the mouth of God." (Matthew 4:4)
2. The devil now takes Jesus up into the holy city (Jerusalem) and challenges Jesus to exalt Himself. I must interject this thought. There are so many men and women of God who has exalted themselves in the Word and work of God. It is a good work, but is it a God work? The God work is what you know God has anointed and appointed you to do. If you exalt your own self, Satan has taken you to the top and he will watch you fall. Wait on the Lord and in due season He will exalt you.

    The tempter took Jesus to the pinnacle of the temple. After Satan had taken Him to the top, he challenged Him to prove

He was called by God. "…If thou be the Son of God…" When you encounter anyone demanding you to prove who you are in Christ; that is an anti-Christ Spirit. We are not here to prove who we are. We are here to prove who Jesus, the Son of God is. "Jesus said unto him, It is written again, Thou shalt not tempt the Lord thy God." (Matthew 4:7)

3. The devil still has not had enough of being defeated with the Word of God. "Again, the devil taketh him up into an exceeding high mountain, and sheweth him all the kingdoms of the world, and the glory of them." (Matthew 4:8)

Sin is only good for a season. Now, the devil shows Jesus the world. Notice he only shows Him the glory of all the world and all the kingdoms of the world.

In all of the world's splendor and beauty, Jesus prophesies later what was going to take place in the end. In Matthew 24:1-2 we read of the end results of the temple and the glory of the world kingdoms. It reads…

> *"And Jesus went out, and departed from the temple: and his disciples came to him for to shew him the buildings of the temple. And Jesus said unto them, See ye not all these things? verily I say unto you, There shall not be left here one stone upon another, that shall not be thrown down."*

We will have an intensive study on the failing kingdoms of this world versus the kingdom of God. The kingdom of God is an everlasting kingdom; a kingdom that will have no end.

Satan reveals his motive in Matthew 4:9 which reads,

> *"…All these things will I give thee, if thou wilt fall down and worship me."*

Every time you do not do what you know is not pleasing to God, you are worshipping Satan. Worship is not only lifting up the name of Jesus; but it is honoring Jesus in our obedience to Him and our daily life style. Never forget when you have sinned or come short to the glory of God, the blood of Jesus will cleanse you and God's grace and mercy will cover you.

When Satan tries to get you to disobey the Word of God and to fall down and worship him, follow Jesus' example and decree as Jesus did in Matthew 4:10-11…

> *"Then saith Jesus unto him, Get thee hence, Satan: for it is written, Thou shalt worship the Lord thy God, and him only shalt thou serve. Then the devil leaveth him, and, behold, angels came and ministered unto him."*

JESUS CHRIST BEGINS
HIS PUBLIC MINISTRY

Matthew 4:12-13

"Now when Jesus had heard that John was cast into prison, he departed into Galilee; And leaving Nazareth, he came and dwelt in Capernaum, which is upon the sea coast, in the borders of Zabulon and Nephthalim."

The Seventh Old Testament Prophecy Being Fulfilled

The prophet Isaiah prophesied in Isaiah 9:1-2 and also in Isaiah 42:6-7 which reads…

Isaiah 9:1-2

"Nevertheless the dimness shall not be such as was in her vexation, when at the first he lightly afflicted the land of Zebulun and the land of Naphtali, and afterward did more grievously afflict her by the way of the sea, beyond Jordan, in Galilee of the nations. The people that walked in darkness have seen a great light: they that dwell in the land of the shadow of death, upon them hath the light shined."

Isaiah 42:6-7

"I the LORD have called thee in righteousness, and will hold thine hand, and will keep thee, and give thee for a covenant of the people, for a light of the Gentiles; To open the blind eyes, to bring out the prisoners from the prison, and them that sit in darkness out of the prison house."

Almost 700 years later, the prophecy is being fulfilled. In Matthew 4:14-17, we read…

"That it might be fulfilled which was spoken by Esaias the prophet, saying, The land of Zabulon, and the land of Nephthalim, by the way of the sea, beyond Jordan, Galilee of the Gentiles; The people

which sat in darkness saw great light; and to them which sat in the region and shadow of death light is sprung up. From that time Jesus began to preach, and to say, Repent: for the kingdom of heaven is at hand."

Keep in mind, if God watched over His Word to make sure every prophecy came to pass yesterday; He will watch over His Word and bring it to pass today. "Jesus Christ the same yesterday, and to day, and for ever." (Hebrews 13:8)

As the Word and work of God began to grow, Jesus begins calling disciples to help Him. Disciples are students who learn the Word and work of God. We read in Matthew 4:18-25…

"And Jesus, walking by the sea of Galilee, saw two brethren, Simon called Peter, and Andrew his brother, casting a net into the sea: for they were fishers. And he saith unto them, Follow me, and I will make you fishers of men. And they straightway left their nets, and followed him. And going on from thence, he saw other two brethren, James the son of Zebedee, and John his brother, in a ship with Zebedee their father, mending their nets; and he called them. And they immediately left the ship and their father, and followed him. And Jesus went about all Galilee, teaching in their synagogues, and preaching the gospel of the kingdom, and healing all manner of sickness and all manner of disease among the people. And his fame went throughout all Syria: and they brought unto him all sick people that were taken with divers diseases and torments, and those which were possessed with devils, and those which were lunatick, and those that had the palsy; and he healed them. And there followed him great multitudes of people from Galilee, and from Decapolis, and from Jerusalem, and from Judaea, and from beyond Jordan."

MATTHEW CHAPTER FOUR
DISCIPLESHIP, LEADERSHIP, MINISTRY
& BIBLE COLLEGE STUDY QUESTIONS

1. Every Christian will be tempted by the devil just as Jesus was tempted. Give five things Jesus did to be prepared when the devil came to tempt Him?

1._____

2._____

3._____

4._____

5._____

2. What was the first temptation Jesus had to overcome?

_____

3. What was that temptation a type and shadow of?

_____

_____

_____

4. What did Jesus do when He heard John the Baptist was in prison?

_____

_____

5. Why do you think Jesus did not go to deliver John from prison?

_____

_____

6. What is the gospel of the kingdom? _____

_____

MATTHEW CHAPTER FOUR
YOUTH & TEEN STUDY QUESTIONS

Name_____ Date _____ Grade_____

1. Did you read chapter four?_____

2. Do you know what it means to be tempted?_____

3. Write your definition for tempted _____
_____

4. Have you ever been tempted? _____

5. When the tempted came to you, did you make the right choice?
_____
(There are always consequences for every action)

6. Read Matthew 4:1-11 again. How did Jesus defeat Satan when he came to tempt Jesus? _____
_____

7. Jesus gave an example of how to defeat temptations. What did Jesus use to overcome temptations? _____
_____

8. When you are tempted, what three things should you do?
(1)_____
(2)_____
(3)_____

MATTHEW CHAPTER FIVE
THE MOUNTAIN TOP SERMON

Matthew 5:1-12

"And seeing the multitudes, he went up into a mountain: and when he was set, his disciples came unto him: And he opened his mouth, and taught them, saying, Blessed are the poor in spirit: for theirs is the kingdom of heaven. Blessed are they that mourn: for they shall be comforted. Blessed are the meek: for they shall inherit the earth. Blessed are they which do hunger and thirst after righteousness: for they shall be filled. Blessed are the merciful: for they shall obtain mercy. Blessed are the pure in heart: for they shall see God. Blessed are the peacemakers: for they shall be called the children of God. Blessed are they which are persecuted for righteousness' sake: for theirs is the kingdom of heaven. Blessed are ye, when men shall revile you, and persecute you, and shall say all manner of evil against you falsely, for my sake. Rejoice, and be exceeding glad: for great is your reward in heaven: for so persecuted they the prophets which were before you."

There are nine "blessed" in verses three (which stands for resurrection into a new life style and a new way of living) through ten. Notice, Matthew writes in the past tense. He is reminding us of the victory Jesus has gained for us in chapter three. Now, you must not allow the devil to come in and steal your joy and peace in God.

The word "blessed" means you are to be "happy and joyful" because you have faith in the Word of God to perform and bring to pass all the promises of God. You are blessed and prosperous because of whose you are. You are a child of the Most High God and what God has promised you, He will do. Briefly – Blessed is joyful and happy.

Now, that you know whose you are and what you are to expect, you can rejoice in the Lord always.

Christians Are To Be The Similitude's of Christ In The World. Jesus begins His message with these words in Matthew 5:13-16…

"Ye are the salt of the earth: but if the salt have lost his savour, wherewith shall it be salted? it is thenceforth good for nothing, but to be cast out, and to be trodden under foot of men. Ye are the light of the world. A city that is set on an hill cannot be hid. Neither do men light a candle, and put it under a bushel, but on a candlestick; and it giveth light unto all that are in the house. Let your light so shine before men, that they may see your good works, and glorify your Father which is in heaven."

Salt is a preservative and is used to season and enhance the flavor. Whenever there is darkness, light is needed. It does not matter how small you think your light is; there will always be a dark place in the world that need your light. "Let your light so shine before men, that they may see your good works, and glorify your Father which is in heaven." (Matthew 5:16)

The Law And Our Lord Jesus Christ

Matthew 5:17-30

"Think not that I am come to destroy the law, or the prophets: I am not come to destroy, but to fulfil. For verily I say unto you, Till heaven and earth pass, one jot or one tittle shall in no wise pass from the law, till all be fulfilled. Whosoever therefore shall break one of these least commandments, and shall teach men so, he shall be called the least in the kingdom of heaven: but whosoever shall do and teach them, the same shall be called great in the kingdom of heaven. For I say unto you, That except your righteousness shall exceed the righteousness of the scribes and Pharisees, ye shall in no case enter into the kingdom of heaven. Ye have heard that it was said by them of old time, Thou shalt not kill; and whosoever shall kill shall be in danger of the judgment: But I say unto you, That whosoever is angry with his brother without a cause shall be in danger of the judgment: and whosoever shall say to his brother, Raca, shall be in danger of the council: but whosoever shall say, Thou fool, shall be in danger of hell fire. Therefore if thou bring thy gift to the altar, and there rememberest that thy brother hath ought against thee; Leave there thy gift before the altar, and go thy way; first be reconciled to thy brother, and then come and offer thy gift. Agree with thine adversary quickly, whiles thou art in the way with him; lest at any

time the adversary deliver thee to the judge, and the judge deliver thee to the officer, and thou be cast into prison. Verily I say unto thee, Thou shalt by no means come out thence, till thou hast paid the uttermost farthing. Ye have heard that it was said by them of old time, Thou shalt not commit adultery: But I say unto you, That whosoever looketh on a woman to lust after her hath committed adultery with her already in his heart. And if thy right eye offend thee, pluck it out, and cast it from thee: for it is profitable for thee that one of thy members should perish, and not that thy whole body should be cast into hell. And if thy right hand offend thee, cut if off, and cast it from thee: for it is profitable for thee that one of thy members should perish, and not that thy whole body should be cast into hell."

The New Law Of The Lord

Matthew 5:31-48

"It hath been said, Whosoever shall put away his wife, let him give her a writing of divorcement: But I say unto you, That whosoever shall put away his wife, saving for the cause of fornication, causeth her to commit adultery: and whosoever shall marry her that is divorced committeth adultery. Again, ye have heard that it hath been said by them of old time, Thou shalt not forswear thyself, but shalt perform unto the Lord thine oaths: But I say unto you, Swear not at all; neither by heaven; for it is God's throne: Nor by the earth; for it is his footstool: neither by Jerusalem; for it is the city of the great King. Neither shalt thou swear by thy head, because thou canst not make one hair white or black. But let your communication be, Yea, yea; Nay, nay: for whatsoever is more than these cometh of evil. Ye have heard that it hath been said, An eye for an eye, and a tooth for a tooth: But I say unto you, That ye resist not evil: but whosoever shall smite thee on thy right cheek, turn to him the other also. And if any man will sue thee at the law, and take away thy coat, let him have thy cloke also. And whosoever shall compel thee to go a mile, go with him twain. Give to him that asketh thee, and from him that would borrow of thee turn not thou away. Ye have heard that it hath been said, Thou shalt love thy neighbour, and hate thine enemy. But I say unto you, Love your enemies, bless them that curse you, do good to them that hate you, and pray for them which despitefully

use you, and persecute you; That ye may be the children of your Father which is in heaven: for he maketh his sun to rise on the evil and on the good, and sendeth rain on the just and on the unjust. For if ye love them which love you, what reward have ye? do not even the publicans the same? And if ye salute your brethren only, what do ye more than others? do not even the publicans so? Be ye therefore perfect, even as your Father which is in heaven is perfect."

The law of the Lord encourages you to be perfect. That word "perfect" does not mean "flawless and free of all sin" (that will take place as you continue to live for Jesus, it's your choice). It means "fully developed, matured using Christ as your example, seek to be like Christ."

MATTHEW CHAPTER FIVE
YOUTH & TEEN STUDY QUESTIONS

Name_____ Date_____ Grade_____

1. What does the word "blessed" mean? _____
_____

2. Are all Christians blessed? _____

3. How many times do you find the word "blessed" in Matthew 5:3-11? _____

4. What should be your response to friends, family members and all those who say all manners of evil against you falsely? _____
_____
_____

5. Have you ever heard the word "blessed" before? _____

6. What do you think that word mean? _____
_____

7. Are you blessed? _____

8. How do you know you are blessed? _____
_____

9. Do you believe you are a mighty boy or girl of God? _____
_____

10. How did Jesus say you are to handle anger? _____
_____

MATTHEW CHAPTER FIVE
DISCIPLESHIP, LEADERSHIP, MINISTRY
& BIBLE COLLEGE STUDY QUESTIONS

1. Define "blessed" _____

2. What are we to hunger and thirst after? _____

3. Jesus said we are the salt of the earth. What does salt do? _____
_____

4. What is the purpose of light? _____

5. How can you keep your light shining? _____
_____

6. Did you complete your summaries? _____

7. Did Jesus come to destroy the law? _____

8. What did Jesus say He had come to do with the law?
_____

9. Under the law of the Lord, what are you to do if have someone angry with you without a cause? _____
_____

10. What are you to do if you are preparing to give your tithes and offerings and you know your brother have ought against you? ____
_____
_____

MATTHEW CHAPTER SIX
YOUR MOTIVES WHEN YOU PRAY

Matthew 6:1-8

"Take heed that ye do not your alms before men, to be seen of them: otherwise ye have no reward of your Father which is in heaven. Therefore when thou doest thine alms, do not sound a trumpet before thee, as the hypocrites do in the synagogues and in the streets, that they may have glory of men. Verily I say unto you, They have their reward. But when thou doest alms, let not thy left hand know what thy right hand doeth: That thine alms may be in secret: and thy Father which seeth in secret himself shall reward thee openly. And when thou prayest, thou shalt not be as the hypocrites are: for they love to pray standing in the synagogues and in the corners of the streets, that they may be seen of men. Verily I say unto you, They have their reward. But thou, when thou prayest, enter into thy closet, and when thou hast shut thy door, pray to thy Father which is in secret; and thy Father which seeth in secret shall reward thee openly. But when ye pray, use not vain repetitions, as the heathen do: for they think that they shall be heard for their much speaking. Be not ye therefore like unto them: for your Father knoweth what things ye have need of, before ye ask him."

God knows what you need before you ask. You might be wondering, why should we pray? When you pray, you are agreeing with God that His will, will be done on earth as it is in heaven.

Jesus said there is a manner to prayer. That manner He reveals in Matthew 6:9-13, which reads…

"After this manner therefore pray ye: Our Father which art in heaven, Hallowed be thy name. Thy kingdom come. Thy will be done in earth, as it is in heaven. Give us this day our daily bread. And forgive us our debts, as we forgive our debtors. And lead us not into temptation, but deliver us from evil: For thine is the kingdom, and the power, and the glory, for ever. Amen."

God's Word is His will. Every born-again Spirit filled Christian is in the world, but they are not of the world. After you were translated out of the kingdom of darkness into the kingdom of God's dear Son, Jesus; you must learn to live like a king's child.

Jesus said, "…in the world you shall have tribulation…" but you must be of good cheer for He has overcome the world. (John 16:33) That overcoming power demonstrated the kingdom of God. When the world observed our positional stance in Christ, regardless of our condition, they will know we are children of the kingdom of God. We are anointed and appointed by God to reveal His kingdom as it comes and let His will be done.

"Give us this day our daily bread." (Matthew 6:11) Daily, God will supply all your needs according to His riches in glory by Christ Jesus.

Matthew 6:12
"And forgive us our debts, as we forgive our debtors."

There is power in forgiveness. When you forgive someone for the hurt and pain they have caused you; you not only bring deliverance to them, but you free yourself. You free yourself from the prison of disappointment, condemnation and unrealistic expectations of you. It is God, who will send a spirit of peace and rest upon you.

Matthew 6:13-15

"And lead us not into temptation, but deliver us from evil: For thine is the kingdom, and the power, and the glory, for ever. Amen. For if ye forgive men their trespasses, your heavenly Father will also forgive you: But if ye forgive not men their trespasses, neither will your Father forgive your trespasses."

WHEN YOU FAST

Matthew 6:16-18

"Moreover when ye fast, be not, as the hypocrites, of a sad countenance: for they disfigure their faces, that they may appear

unto men to fast. Verily I say unto you, They have their reward. But thou, when thou fastest, anoint thine head, and wash thy face; That thou appear not unto men to fast, but unto thy Father which is in secret: and thy Father, which seeth in secret, shall reward thee openly."

Fasting is to abstain from food and water for a certain length of time. Isaiah 58:4-7 is where Isaiah writes about fasting. There are at least two types of fasts I have found in the Bible that our church has gone on. One is the Daniel fast listed in Daniel 1:8-12. The end results were Daniel 1:17-20.

The second one, I called the Jesus fast. In this fast, you do not eat or drink anything. This is the fast Jesus was on when He went into the wilderness to be tempted by the devil. When you are led to fast, pray and ask God how long should you fast. God will direct your steps. During your fast, pray and study the Word of God. Your spirit will be fed.

Matthew 6:19-34

"Lay not up for yourselves treasures upon earth, where moth and rust doth corrupt, and where thieves break through and steal: But lay up for yourselves treasures in heaven, where neither moth nor rust doth corrupt, and where thieves do not break through nor steal: For where your treasure is, there will your heart be also. The light of the body is the eye: if therefore thine eye be single, thy whole body shall be full of light. But if thine eye be evil, thy whole body shall be full of darkness. If therefore the light that is in thee be darkness, how great is that darkness! No man can serve two masters: for either he will hate the one, and love the other; or else he will hold to the one, and despise the other. Ye cannot serve God and mammon. Therefore I say unto you, Take no thought for your life, what ye shall eat, or what ye shall drink; nor yet for your body, what ye shall put on. Is not the life more than meat, and the body than raiment? Behold the fowls of the air: for they sow not, neither do they reap, nor gather into barns; yet your heavenly Father feedeth them. Are ye not much better than they? Which of you by taking thought can add one cubit unto his stature? And why

take ye thought for raiment? Consider the lilies of the field, how they grow; they toil not, neither do they spin: And yet I say unto you, That even Solomon in all his glory was not arrayed like one of these. Wherefore, if God so clothe the grass of the field, which to day is, and to morrow is cast into the oven, shall he not much more clothe you, O ye of little faith? Therefore take no thought, saying, What shall we eat? or, What shall we drink? or, Wherewithal shall we be clothed? (For after all these things do the Gentiles seek:) for your heavenly Father knoweth that ye have need of all these things. But seek ye first the kingdom of God, and his righteousness; and all these things shall be added unto you. Take therefore no thought for the morrow: for the morrow shall take thought for the things of itself. Sufficient unto the day is the evil thereof."

Our desires should be to seek His kingdom first. If we would see those things that Jesus sought after while here on earth; God will add to us as He did to His Son, Jesus.

In Romans 14:17-18 Paul writes…

"For the kingdom of God is not meat and drink; but righteousness, and peace, and joy in the Holy Ghost. For he that in these things serveth Christ is acceptable to God, and approved of men."

The kingdom of God is manifested through your righteous life style. Daily, you must "…seek ye first the kingdom of God, and his righteousness; and all these things shall be added unto you." (Matthew 6:33)

MATTHEW CHAPTER SIX
YOUTH & TEEN STUDY QUESTIONS

Name_____ Date_____ Grade_____

1. Do you begin your day with prayer? _____

2. Name three prayer requests you talk to God about each day?
(1)_____
(2)_____
(3)_____

3. Did you know you can tell God everything that has been troubling you? _____

4. What is fasting? _____

5. Name the young man in your Bible Study Lesson who fast? _____
_____

6. Why did the young man fast? _____

7. In chapter six, what did Jesus teach that you liked the most? _____
_____
_____

8. What did you learn from chapter six that will help you be a better Christian? _____
_____
_____

MATTHEW CHAPTER SIX
DISCIPLESHIP, LEADERSHIP, MINISTRY
& BIBLE COLLEGE STUDY QUESTIONS

1. Who did Jesus say will have their reward when they give? _____
_____

2. Did you read and did you understand chapter six? _____

3. To whom did Jesus say we are to address our prayers? _____
_____

4. Give three applications you learned from the Lord's Prayer that you can apply to your daily life.
(1)_____
(2)_____
(3)_____

5. What lesson did Jesus teach you about forgiveness?
_____
_____
_____

6. What lesson did Jesus teach you about fasting?
_____
_____
_____

7. What did Jesus teach you about taking thought for tomorrow? __
_____

MATTHEW CHAPTER SEVEN
JUDGE NOT

Matthew 7:1-6

"Judge not, that ye be not judged. For with what judgment ye judge, ye shall be judged: and with what measure ye mete, it shall be measured to you again. And why beholdest thou the mote that is in thy brother's eye, but considerest not the beam that is in thine own eye? Or how wilt thou say to thy brother, Let me pull out the mote out of thine eye; and, behold, a beam is in thine own eye? Thou hypocrite, first cast out the beam out of thine own eye; and then shalt thou see clearly to cast out the mote out of thy brother's eye. Give not that which is holy unto the dogs, neither cast ye your pearls before swine, lest they trample them under their feet, and turn again and rend you."

When we look at ourselves first, we will find ourselves coming short of the glory of God. God loves us so much until He sent Jesus to teach us God's Word. In the Word of God, we will find God's principles for living a victorious Christian life.

Chapter seven begins with us examining our self. You are not to examine yourself to condemn yourself. You must examine yourself because you love God and you want to please God by obeying His Word.

ASK GOD FOR HELP

Matthew 7:7-12

"Ask, and it shall be given you; seek, and ye shall find; knock, and it shall be opened unto you: For every one that asketh receiveth; and he that seeketh findeth; and to him that knocketh it shall be opened. Or what man is there of you, whom if his son ask bread, will he give him a stone? Or if he ask a fish, will he give him a serpent? If ye then, being evil, know how to give good gifts unto your children, how much more shall your Father which is in heaven give good things to them that ask him? Therefore all things whatsoever ye

would that men should do to you, do ye even so to them: for this is the law and the prophets."

Jesus is teaching you how to live a more abundant Christian life. In John 10:10, it reads, "The thief cometh not, but for to steal, and to kill, and to destroy: I am come that they might have life, and that they might have it more abundantly."

To give you a clearer understanding of what Jesus is saying, I will also use the Amplified translation of John 10:10 which reads, "The thief comes only in order to steal and kill and destroy. I came that they may have and enjoy life, and have it in abundance (to the full, till it overflows)."

Reading that Scripture in the Amplified Bible let me know we, as apostles, prophets, evangelists, pastors and teachers; have our jobs cut out for us by Jesus. It is not the perfect will of God that one of His children does not live an abundant Christian life.

Jesus does not deny there is a thief. As a matter of fact, He warns us of a thief and how we are to recognize if he has slipped in. Jesus came and He brought every born-again Holy Ghost filled Christian joy, peace and He gave us the measure of faith. Also in 2 Peter 1:3-4, we read…

> *"According as his divine power hath given unto us all things that pertain unto life and godliness, through the knowledge of him that hath called us to glory and virtue: Whereby are given unto us exceeding great and precious promises: that by these ye might be partakers of the divine nature, having escaped the corruption that is in the world through lust."*

When you lack the fullness of joy, peace, the fullness of victory, the fullness of power to overcome every attack of the devil; the thief has come in and stolen from you. If a thief is caught, he must restore seven-fold.

The way you catch a thief is with the weapons of God's Word. The thief came to Jesus to tempt Him while He was going through the wilderness of tests and trials. Jesus overcame him by the power of the Holy Ghost and the Word of God.

We do not minimize the fact that Jesus was the Son of God with power; but when He came in the flesh, He suffered like every one of us suffered in the flesh. He was tempted as we are tempted, but He was without sin. (Hebrews 4:15).

It is Jesus' perfect will that every child of God learn to live an abundant life. God did not send one of the prophets to teach us how to live an abundant life. God sent His only begotten Son to demonstrate to us, with the help of God we could do all things.

Jesus called ordinary men to become His disciples. These men, all with different backgrounds, wrote what they saw and what Jesus said. Jesus impacted their lives with what He said and did. Until after His death, they began to do what He did. They began to turn the world upside down for Jesus.

Through the power of the Holy Ghost, your knowledge and faith in the Word of God; you, too, can do all things through Christ who will strengthen you.

Those men of God, who wrote what they saw Jesus do, believed they could continue to follow Jesus' example until they had finished their course. Now, they are in the presence of God.

In Matthew chapter one through chapter seven, Jesus has been revealing to us the process and the tests you must undergo before you are ready and prepared for the Lord. The disciples were made ready by Jesus and they were prepared to teach others to live an abundant life.

Jesus continues teaching kingdom principles for an Abundant Christian Life. You will find a sub-topic for each teaching. These topics should assist you in targeting all areas you might need to become empowered or restored in. Allow Holy Spirit to restore you.

ENTER YE IN AT THE STRAIGHT GATE
(Salvation Is A Requirement)

Matthew 7:13-14

"Enter ye in at the strait gate: for wide is the gate, and broad is the way, that leadeth to destruction, and many there be which go in thereat: Because strait is the gate, and narrow is the way, which leadeth unto life, and few there be that find it."

BEWARE OF FALSE PROPHETS

Matthew 7:15-20

"Beware of false prophets, which come to you in sheep's clothing, but inwardly they are ravening wolves. Ye shall know them by their fruits. Do men gather grapes of thorns, or figs of thistles? Even so every good tree bringeth forth good fruit; but a corrupt tree bringeth forth evil fruit. A good tree cannot bring forth evil fruit, neither can a corrupt tree bring forth good fruit. Every tree that bringeth not forth good fruit is hewn down, and cast into the fire. Wherefore by their fruits ye shall know them."

You can be religious and be lost. Religious people do not see the need to produce fruit. You must be planted in the Lord. To be planted in the Lord is to be rooted and grounded in God's Word. You are like a tree planted by the rivers of water and you refuse to allow anyone or anything to move you from the Word of God. In due season, you will bring forth the fruit of the Spirit in Galatians 5:22-23, which reads…

"But the fruit of the Spirit is love, joy, peace, longsuffering, gentleness, goodness, faith, Meekness, temperance: against such there is no law."

This I say then, Walk in the Spirit.

TO BE RELIGIOUS WITHOUT CHRIST IS TO BE LOST

Matthew 7:21-23

"Not every one that saith unto me, Lord, Lord, shall enter into the kingdom of heaven; but he that doeth the will of my Father which is in heaven. Many will say to me in that day, Lord, Lord, have we not prophesied in thy name? and in thy name have cast out devils? and in thy name done many wonderful works? And then will I profess unto them, I never knew you: depart from me, ye that work iniquity."

There are many religious people who attend church faithfully every Sunday. They are faithful with their tithes and offerings and they attend Bible Study; but they have never had a personal relationship with Jesus Christ.

The Apostle Paul was the same way until he came in contact with Jesus Christ. After he had a personal encounter with Jesus Christ, he stopped being religious and began a life of fellowship and love for Jesus. He did not preach and teach God's Word out of duty; but he did it for his passionate love for Christ which produced a desire. That same Jesus is present with you now and He desires fellowship with you.

EXERCISE SOUND JUDGEMENT (Don't Build On Sand)

Matthew 7:24-29

"Therefore whosoever heareth these sayings of mine, and doeth them, I will liken him unto a wise man, which built his house upon a rock: And the rain descended, and the floods came, and the winds blew, and beat upon that house; and it fell not: for it was founded upon a rock. And every one that heareth these sayings of mine, and doeth them not, shall be likened unto a foolish man, which built his house upon the sand: And the rain descended, and the floods came, and the winds blew, and beat upon that house; and it fell: and great was the fall of it. And it came to pass, when Jesus had ended these sayings, the people were astonished at his doctrine: For he taught them as one having authority, and not as the scribes."

MATTHEW CHAPTER SEVEN
YOUTH & TEEN STUDY QUESTIONS

Name_____ Date_____ Grade_____

1. Did you read chapter seven? _____

2. Have you judged someone before you were able to get to know them? (The word "judge" means "to decide beforehand, to make a conclusion.") _____

3. Have someone judged you before they asked you what had happened? _____

4. How did it make you feel? _____
_____

5. Jesus knew all of us would be judged falsely. So, I believe He took time out of His busy schedule to write Matthew 7:1-5. (Read it. Then ask God to help you forgive the person who judged you falsely.) Now, how do you feel? _____
_____

6. What is the law and the prophets? _____
_____
(This is truly a good law. We should do unto others as we would have them do unto us.)

7. Have you received Jesus into your heart? _____

8. Have you been baptized in the Holy Ghost? _____
(If your answer is "no" ask your teacher to pray with you."

MATTHEW CHAPTER SEVEN
DISCIPLESHIP, LEADERSHIP, MINISTRY
& BIBLE COLLEGE STUDY QUESTIONS

1. Did you complete your summaries of chapter seven? _____

2. What did Jesus teach about judging? _____
_____

3. When Jesus said, "Ask and it shall be given you…" what was Jesus referring to? _____

4. As a Disciple, Leader or Minister of Jesus Christ, who did Jesus say you should be aware of? _____

5. What are the signs of false prophets? _____
_____

6. What is the difference between a religious person and a righteous person? _____
_____

7. Who are workers of iniquity? _____

8. What did Jesus say would be His response to those who did not profess Christ? _____

9. Who will enter the kingdom of heaven? _____

10. Are you a born-again Christian? _____

11. Have you received the baptism in the Holy Ghost? _____

MATTHEW CHAPTER EIGHT
KING JESUS HAS POWER OVER DEFILEMENT –
MIRACLES BEGIN

Matthew 8:1-4

"When he was come down from the mountain, great multitudes followed him. And, behold, there came a leper and worshipped him, saying, Lord, if thou wilt, thou canst make me clean. And Jesus put forth his hand, and touched him, saying, I will; be thou clean. And immediately his leprosy was cleansed. And Jesus saith unto him, See thou tell no man; but go thy way, shew thyself to the priest, and offer the gift that Moses commanded, for a testimony unto them."

No one miracle had been recorded of anyone being healed of leprosy in over a thousand years. This miracle had an impact on the priest. Jesus demonstrated the kingdom of God was among them.

In the Lord's Prayer in Matthew 6:10, it reads, "Thy kingdom come…" Jesus was the kingdom of God among them. God's will was being done. It was not the will of God for anyone to be sick. The devil came, after the fall of Adam and Eve, to kill, steal and destroy with sickness and death. Jesus came to destroy the works of the devil.

The kings who are in the world and from the world operate by the world system from a worldly throne. Then, King Jesus came into the world to reveal what a kingdom of God rule was all about. King Jesus did not come to rule from the outside in, but from the inside out. He came to set up His throne in our hearts giving us the same power He had through the infilling of the Holy Ghost. Jesus demonstrated power over the defilement of the body.

Secondly, Jesus Demonstrated He Had Power Over Distance With The Healing Of The Centurion's Servant.

Matthew 8:5-13

"And when Jesus was entered into Capernaum, there came unto

him a centurion, beseeching him, And saying, Lord, my servant lieth at home sick of the palsy, grievously tormented. And Jesus saith unto him, I will come and heal him. The centurion answered and said, Lord, I am not worthy that thou shouldest come under my roof: but speak the word only, and my servant shall be healed. For I am a man under authority, having soldiers under me: and I say to this man, Go, and he goeth; and to another, Come, and he cometh; and to my servant, Do this, and he doeth it. When Jesus heard it, he marvelled, and said to them that followed, Verily I say unto you, I have not found so great faith, no, not in Israel. And I say unto you, That many shall come from the east and west, and shall sit down with Abraham, and Isaac, and Jacob, in the kingdom of heaven. But the children of the kingdom shall be cast out into outer darkness: there shall be weeping and gnashing of teeth. And Jesus said unto the centurion, Go thy way; and as thou hast believed, so be it done unto thee. And his servant was healed in the selfsame hour."

A centurion is a Roman army officer who had about 100 men he was in charge of. With all his delegated authority from man, he did not have power to heal his servant. Only Jesus Christ possesses all power and authority of a King. There are no limits to Jesus' power and authority. He not only has the power to rule in the earth, but He also has power over the heavens.

Jesus now heals Peter's mother-in-law.

Matthew 8:14-15

"And when Jesus was come into Peter's house, he saw his wife's mother laid, and sick of a fever. And he touched her hand, and the fever left her: and she arose, and ministered unto them."

Kings of the earth touched with a scepter, not their hand, to demonstrate their power. Jesus, the King of kings, touched with His hand. When He touched Peter's mother-in-law, it was the hand of God bringing restoration. "When the even was come, they brought unto him many that were possessed with devils: and he cast out the spirits with his word, and healed all that were sick." (Matthew 8:16)

The Eighth Old Testament Prophecy Being Fulfilled in Isaiah 53:1-5

Matthew 8:17-18

"That it might be fulfilled which was spoken by Esaias the prophet, saying, Himself took our infirmities, and bare our sicknesses. Now when Jesus saw great multitudes about him, he gave commandment to depart unto the other side."

"Follow Me" – The Sacrifice, The Separation For The Savior

Matthew 8:19-22

"And a certain scribe came, and said unto him, Master, I will follow thee whithersoever thou goest. And Jesus saith unto him, The foxes have holes, and the birds of the air have nests; but the Son of man hath not where to lay his head. And another of his disciples said unto him, Lord, suffer me first to go and bury my father. But Jesus said unto him, Follow me; and let the dead bury their dead."

The King Has Power Over The Deep – Jesus Stills The Storm

Matthew 8:23-27

"And when he was entered into a ship, his disciples followed him. And, behold, there arose a great tempest in the sea, insomuch that the ship was covered with the waves: but he was asleep. And his disciples came to him, and awoke him, saying, Lord, save us: we perish. And he saith unto them, Why are ye fearful, O ye of little faith? Then he arose, and rebuked the winds and the sea; and there was a great calm. But the men marvelled, saying, What manner of man is this, that even the winds and the sea obey him!"

Jesus is King over the storms. Not only is He the King and ruler over the stormy seas, but He can also rule over every storm of your natural life. You must have faith in Him that He can and will calm the storms of life.

Now, Jesus Demonstrates The Power Of The King Over Demons, Even

Demons Are Subject To The Son Of God – He Has All Power

Matthew 8:28-34

"And when he was come to the other side into the country of the Gergesenes, there met him two possessed with devils, coming out of the tombs, exceeding fierce, so that no man might pass by that way. And, behold, they cried out, saying, What have we to do with thee, Jesus, thou Son of God? art thou come hither to torment us before the time? And there was a good way off from them an herd of many swine feeding. So the devils besought him, saying, If thou cast us out, suffer us to go away into the herd of swine. And he said unto them, Go. And when they were come out, they went into the herd of swine: and, behold, the whole herd of swine ran violently down a steep place into the sea, and perished in the waters. And they that kept them fled, and went their ways into the city, and told every thing, and what was befallen to the possessed of the devils. And, behold, the whole city came out to meet Jesus: and when they saw him, they besought him that he would depart out of their coasts."

The demons knew Jesus was the Son of God and they knew they could not overthrow the King. They also knew they would one day be cast into a lake of fire and be tormented day and night for all the torment they had brought to earth and to the children of God. They also knew God loved the world and the people so much until it was not His will that any be lost. So, God was giving all mankind time to receive His Son, Jesus, into their lives.

With that in mind, my question to you is "Are you making sure you are telling everyone you know, who has not given their life to Jesus Christ, to receive Him?" I pray you are not one who is causing Jesus to delay His soon return.

116

MATTHEW CHAPTER EIGHT
YOUTH & TEEN STUDY QUESTIONS

Name_____ Date_____ Grade_____

1. Did you read chapter eight?_____

2. Do you know what a miracle is?_____

3. Have you ever seen a miracle?_____

4. If your answer is "yes" write the miracle down that you saw. _____
_____

5. Who is the only one that can perform a miracle? _____

6. What was the first miracle Jesus performed in Matthew? _____
_____

7. Do you know what it means to be healed? _____

8. Ask your parent or teacher to explain to you the difference in healing and miracles. Write the answer down._____
_____
_____

9. Do you know what "faith" is?_____

10. What is "faith?"_____
_____
_____

MATTHEW CHAPTER EIGHT
DISCIPLESHIP, LEADERSHIP, MINISTRY
& BIBLE COLLEGE STUDY QUESTIONS

1. What was the first miracle Jesus performed in chapter eight? ____
_____

2. What did the leper do to get Jesus' attention? _____
_____

3. Read Matthew 8:7 – When Jesus was asked to come to the centurion's house to pray for his servant, how and when did Jesus prepare Himself? _____
_____
_____

4. Have you prepared yourself to heal those who you come in contact with or do you call your pastor or spiritual leader? _____
_____

5. How do you see faith manifested in this chapter? _____
_____

6. What was the third miracle Jesus performed in Matthew? _____
_____

7. What was the Old Testament prophecy fulfilled in Matthew? ____
_____

8. Who came to Jesus and said they would follow Jesus wherever He would go? _____
_____

9. What excuse did the second disciple give? _____
_____

10. Did you complete your summaries?_____

MATTHEW CHAPTER NINE
THAT YE MAY KNOW THAT THE SON OF MAN HATH POWER ON EARTH

JESUS HEALS A PALSIED MAN

Matthew 9:1-8

"And he entered into a ship, and passed over, and came into his own city. And, behold, they brought to him a man sick of the palsy, lying on a bed: and Jesus seeing their faith said unto the sick of the palsy; Son, be of good cheer; thy sins be forgiven thee. And, behold, certain of the scribes said within themselves, This man blasphemeth. And Jesus knowing their thoughts said, Wherefore think ye evil in your hearts? For whether is easier, to say, Thy sins be forgiven thee; or to say, Arise, and walk? But that ye may know that the Son of man hath power on earth to forgive sins, (then saith he to the sick of the palsy,) Arise, take up thy bed, and go unto thine house. And he arose, and departed to his house. But when the multitudes saw it, they marvelled, and glorified God, which had given such power unto men."

I AM NOT COME TO CALL THE RIGHTEOUS, BUT SINNERS TO REPENTANCE

Matthew 9:9-15

"And as Jesus passed forth from thence, he saw a man, named Matthew, sitting at the receipt of custom: and he saith unto him, Follow me. And he arose, and followed him. And it came to pass, as Jesus sat at meat in the house, behold, many publicans and sinners came and sat down with him and his disciples. And when the Pharisees saw it, they said unto his disciples, Why eateth your Master with publicans and sinners? But when Jesus heard that, he said unto them, They that be whole need not a physician, but they that are sick. But go ye and learn what that meaneth, I will have mercy, and not sacrifice: for I am not come to call the righteous, but sinners to repentance. Then came to him the disciples of John, saying, Why do we and the Pharisees fast oft, but thy disciples

fast not? And Jesus said unto them, Can the children of the bridechamber mourn, as long as the bridegroom is with them? but the days will come, when the bridegroom shall be taken from them, and then shall they fast."

The Jews who were employed by the Roman government to collect taxes were known as publicans. The people did not think highly of them, they were considered as traders and many of them were dishonest. Unlike many Christians today, Jesus came to call the publicans and sinners to repentance.

Jesus did not allow their comments to cause His to lose sight of His mission and His ministry. The religious leaders were speaking evil of Him. Jesus saw them as sin-sick sinners who needed a physician.

Sin is like leprosy and cancer. It begins small but it doesn't take long for it to spread. When the disease spreads, it begins to affect other areas of the body.

Jesus is the only One who can heal a sin-sick soul. But when healing and deliverance take place, Jesus calls the sinner to repentance. When repentance takes place, Jesus cleanses and makes that life new.

PUT NEW WINE INTO NEW BOTTLES AND BOTH ARE PRESERVED

Matthew 9:16-19

"No man putteth a piece of new cloth unto an old garment, for that which is put in to fill it up taketh from the garment, and the rent is made worse. Neither do men put new wine into old bottles: else the bottles break, and the wine runneth out, and the bottles perish: but they put new wine into new bottles, and both are preserved. While he spake these things unto them, behold, there came a certain ruler, and worshipped him, saying, My daughter is even now dead: but come and lay thy hand upon her, and she shall live. And Jesus arose, and followed him, and so did his disciples."

Jesus speaks of new bottles and new wines. I believe Jesus is using this parable to give understanding to those who were sinners, but they repented and ask Jesus into their lives. Jesus cleans from the inside out. The Scribes and Pharisees looked at the outside. They judge by the seeing of the eye; but God judges the heart.

While Jesus was teaching, a ruler came and he began worshipping Jesus before he told Him the condition of his daughter. To worship Jesus first is to place Him above every need in our lives. Worship caused Jesus to follow the man. Jesus called for Matthew to follow Him. Now, worship drew Jesus away from the banquet and He followed a man.

The power of God in prayer, worship and His Word will cause Jesus to follow us into the place of our need.

THY FAITH HATH MADE THEE WHOLE

Matthew 9:20-22

"And, behold, a woman, which was diseased with an issue of blood twelve years, came behind him, and touched the hem of his garment: For she said within herself, If I may but touch his garment, I shall be whole. But Jesus turned him about, and when he saw her, he said, Daughter, be of good comfort; thy faith hath made thee whole. And the woman was made whole from that hour."

Jesus is our healer, but Jesus saw a faith in that woman to go beyond healing and be whole. She touched Jesus to be whole. You can be healed and be able to do as this woman did, survive. The woman's faith, when she touched Jesus, caused her to become whole. When you touch the Savior, it is no more survival but wholeness and completeness. Touch Jesus. He will make you whole.

JESUS DEMONSTRATES THE KINGDOM OF GOD IS AMONG US

Matthew 9:23-26

"And when Jesus came into the ruler's house, and saw the minstrels and the people making a noise, He said unto them, Give place: for

the maid is not dead, but sleepeth. And they laughed him to scorn. But when the people were put forth, he went in, and took her by the hand, and the maid arose. And the fame hereof went abroad into all that land."

BELIEVE YE THAT I AM ABLE TO DO THIS?

Matthew 9:27-31

"And when Jesus departed thence, two blind men followed him, crying, and saying, Thou Son of David, have mercy on us. And when he was come into the house, the blind men came to him: and Jesus saith unto them, Believe ye that I am able to do this? They said unto him, Yea, Lord. Then touched he their eyes, saying, According to your faith be it unto you. And their eyes were opened; and Jesus straitly charged them, saying, See that no man know it. But they, when they were departed, spread abroad his fame in all that country."

Jesus first took care of the spiritual sight in this chapter before He healed the two blind men of their natural sight. Jesus asked them a question. (This is the same question He is asking every one of us who get in a dark place in their lives and cannot see their way out.) "…Believe ye that I am able to do this…?" How you answer Jesus will determine how and what you are able to see. Their response was, "Yea, Lord." Jesus said, "According to your faith be it unto you."

THE HARVEST TRULY IS PLENTEOUS, BUT THE LABOURERS ARE FEW

Matthew 9:32-38

"As they went out, behold, they brought to him a dumb man possessed with a devil. And when the devil was cast out, the dumb spake: and the multitudes marvelled, saying, It was never so seen in Israel. But the Pharisees said, He casteth out devils through the prince of the devils. And Jesus went about all the cities and villages, teaching in their synagogues, and preaching the gospel of the kingdom, and healing every sickness and every disease among the people. But when he saw the multitudes, he was moved with

compassion on them, because they fainted, and were scattered abroad, as sheep having no shepherd. Then saith he unto his disciples, The harvest truly is plenteous, but the labourers are few; Pray ye therefore the Lord of the harvest, that he will send forth labourers into his harvest."

Those whom Jesus has opened their eyes to see what He sees will also pray for labourers into the harvest.

MATTHEW CHAPTER NINE
YOUTH & TEEN STUDY QUESTIONS

Name_____ Date_____ Grade_____

1. Do you know what a miracle is? _____

2. Who are you to ask when you need a miracle? _____

3. What did Jesus tell the man who was sick of the palsy?
_____

4. What is "sin?" _____

5. Who can forgive you of all your sins? _____

6. Who was Matthew before he became a disciple of Jesus?
_____

7. What did Jesus call every sinner to do? _____

8. What did Jesus do to the two blind men? _____

9. Have your parents to explain "the harvest truly is plenteous" to you. Ask your parents how both of you can help Jesus with His harvest. Write your answer.
_____
_____

10. Your memory verse is Matthew 9:37. Ask your teacher to sign and date when you learn your verse.

Sign _____ Date_____

MATTHEW CHAPTER NINE
DISCIPLESHIP, LEADERSHIP, MINISTRY
& BIBLE COLLEGE STUDY QUESTIONS

1. What did Jesus see in the man with palsy? _____

2. What gift of the Spirit was operating in Jesus' life? _____
_____

3. There were two areas of the man's life that he needed to be healed in, what were they?
(1)_____
(2)_____

4. What did Jesus desire the Scribes to know? _____
_____

5. Who was Matthew and what was the attitude of the people towards him? _____
_____

6. How does man judge someone? _____

7. How does God judge? _____

8. In chapter nine, there are three messages to prepare you for the Lord, name them.
(1)_____
(2)_____
(3)_____

9. When you meditate upon these three you have listed, tell how they prepared you for the Lord. (Use a sheet of paper).

10. What does it mean to "be whole?" _____
_____

MATTHEW CHAPTER TEN
HE HAD CALLED UNTO HIM
HIS TWELVE DISCIPLES – THE KINGDOM OF HEAVEN IS
AT HAND

Matthew 10:1-15

"And when he had called unto him his twelve disciples, he gave them power against unclean spirits, to cast them out, and to heal all manner of sickness and all manner of disease. Now the names of the twelve apostles are these; The first, Simon, who is called Peter, and Andrew his brother; James the son of Zebedee, and John his brother; Philip, and Bartholomew; Thomas, and Matthew the publican; James the son of Alphaeus, and Lebbaeus, whose surname was Thaddaeus; Simon the Canaanite, and Judas Iscariot, who also betrayed him. These twelve Jesus sent forth, and commanded them, saying, Go not into the way of the Gentiles, and into any city of the Samaritans enter ye not: But go rather to the lost sheep of the house of Israel. And as ye go, preach, saying, The kingdom of heaven is at hand. Heal the sick, cleanse the lepers, raise the dead, cast out devils: freely ye have received, freely give. Provide neither gold, nor silver, nor brass in your purses, Nor scrip for your journey, neither two coats, neither shoes, nor yet staves: for the workman is worthy of his meat. And into whatsoever city or town ye shall enter, inquire who in it is worthy; and there abide till ye go thence. And when ye come into an house, salute it. And if the house be worthy, let your peace come upon it: but if it be not worthy, let your peace return to you. And whosoever shall not receive you, nor hear your words, when ye depart out of that house or city, shake off the dust of your feet. Verily I say unto you, It shall be more tolerable for the land of Sodom and Gomorrha in the day of judgment, than for that city."

PREPARE YOURSELF FOR PERSECUTION

Matthew 10:16-25

"Behold, I send you forth as sheep in the midst of wolves: be ye therefore wise as serpents, and harmless as doves. But beware

of men: for they will deliver you up to the councils, and they will scourge you in their synagogues; And ye shall be brought before governors and kings for my sake, for a testimony against them and the Gentiles. But when they deliver you up, take no thought how or what ye shall speak: for it shall be given you in that same hour what ye shall speak. For it is not ye that speak, but the Spirit of your Father which speaketh in you. And the brother shall deliver up the brother to death, and the father the child: and the children shall rise up against their parents, and cause them to be put to death. And ye shall be hated of all men for my name's sake: but he that endureth to the end shall be saved. But when they persecute you in this city, flee ye into another: for verily I say unto you, Ye shall not have gone over the cities of Israel, till the Son of man be come. The disciple is not above his master, nor the servant above his lord. It is enough for the disciple that he be as his master, and the servant as his lord. If they have called the master of the house Beelzebub, how much more shall they call them of his household?"

Jesus said He was sending His disciples forth as sheep in the midst of wolves. You should not be surprised when you find yourself in the midst of a person who has the characteristic of a wolf. A wolf will move through the sheep quietly and he will try to act like a sheep until he can get close enough to destroy the sheep.

Another tactic of the wolf is to draw the sheep away from the watchful care of the shepherd. That's why Jesus said, "…be ye therefore wise as serpents, and harmless as doves." (Matthew 10:16)

As a disciple of Jesus, you must become wise through the Word of God and the impartation of spiritual mothers and fathers in the gospel, whom God has raised in these last days. You will know them by their fruit; the fruit of revelation, impartation and manifestation of the presence and power of God.

Jesus said you are to be wise. The wisdom of God will demonstrate a godly character and show good judgment. Showing good judgment will cause you to always give God the glory, honor and praise that is due Him. He is Lord and we are His servants.

FEAR YE NOT

Matthew 10:26-31

"Fear them not therefore: for there is nothing covered, that shall not be revealed; and hid, that shall not be known. What I tell you in darkness, that speak ye in light: and what ye hear in the ear, that preach ye upon the housetops. And fear not them which kill the body, but are not able to kill the soul: but rather fear him which is able to destroy both soul and body in hell. Are not two sparrows sold for a farthing? and one of them shall not fall on the ground without your Father. But the very hairs of your head are all numbered. Fear ye not therefore, ye are of more value than many sparrows."

Jesus is saying, "Fear" not. That word "fear" in the Greek is "phobe" which has the meaning of "one who runs away terrified and becomes tighten up." God is with you. You must not forget you are a child of God.

You are being prepared for the Lord just as Jesus prepared His disciples for Himself. He was preparing them for the work they would continue to do after Jesus went back to heaven. In Acts 1:2, Luke wrote, "Until the day in which he was taken up, after that he through the Holy Ghost had given commandments unto the apostles whom he had chosen."

Now we, through the Holy Ghost, must also continue the work Jesus did until He returns.

WE MUST CONTINUE TO CONFESS CHRIST BEFORE MEN

Matthew 10:32-33

"Whosoever therefore shall confess me before men, him will I confess also before my Father which is in heaven. But whosoever shall deny me before men, him will I also deny before my Father which is in heaven."

THERE WILL BE CONFLICT WITH CHANGE

Matthew 10:34-39

"Think not that I am come to send peace on earth: I came not to send peace, but a sword. For I am come to set a man at variance against his father, and the daughter against her mother, and the daughter in law against her mother in law. And a man's foes shall be they of his own household. He that loveth father or mother more than me is not worthy of me: and he that loveth son or daughter more than me is not worthy of me. And he that taketh not his cross, and followeth after me, is not worthy of me. He that findeth his life shall lose it: and he that loseth his life for my sake shall find it."

Take note! Jesus did not say those who are in Christ would not have peace; He left His peace with us. We are in the world, but we are not of the world. Those who are of the world will be like the foolish man who built his life (or house the Bible states in Matthew 7:26) upon the sand. (The sand can be the person who practices sin.) They know what they are doing is an offense to God their heavenly Father; but they continue to do what they are doing. When the tests and trials come, they crumble in the storm.

The child of God built their house, (which is a godly lifestyle built) upon the foundation of God's Word. They do not practice sin; but when they stumble and find themselves doing something that does not please God, they quickly ask God to forgive them. The blood of Jesus begins its work to cleanse them and the power of the Holy Ghost keeps them from falling. They do not practice sin, so they forsake the sin.

Their life is built on the Rock Christ Jesus. He will not let them fall and He will give every Christian the power they need to make it through life's conflicts. After you have gone through the conflicts, God will reward you. As you go forth to continue the work of the Lord, God will reward those who receive the Word of the Lord from you.

This is a special message for every Christian young and old. When the men and women of God receive the Word of God, God has given you to deliver to them. God will bless them for receiving the Word. You know you are a receiver of God's Word when you: (1) Believe God's Word, (2) Receive God's Word and (3) Obey God's Word. You shall be rewarded.

GOD'S REWARD TO YOU

Matthew 10:40-42

"He that receiveth you receiveth me, and he that receiveth me receiveth him that sent me. He that receiveth a prophet in the name of a prophet shall receive a prophet's reward; and he that receiveth a righteous man in the name of a righteous man shall receive a righteous man's reward. And whosoever shall give to drink unto one of these little ones a cup of cold water only in the name of a disciple, verily I say unto you, he shall in no wise lose his reward."

MATTHEW CHAPTER TEN
YOUTH & TEEN STUDY QUESTIONS

Name_____ Date_____ Grade_____

1. Did you read Matthew chapter ten? _____

2. Are you a Christian? _____

3. What is a Christian? _____

4. Have you been baptized in water? _____

5. Why did you get baptized in water? _____

6. If you do not know why you were baptized, ask your parents or your teacher to explain baptism. _____
_____
_____

7. Have you received the Holy Ghost since you believed and received Jesus into your life? _____

8. Do you confess Jesus before your friends? _____

9. If your answer is "yes" how did your friends respond?
_____
_____

If your answer is "no" tell us why you did not tell your friends about Jesus? _____
_____

10. When you became a Christian, did you come into conflict with your friends? _____

MATTHEW CHAPTER TEN
DISCIPLESHIP, LEADERSHIP, MINISTRY
& BIBLE COLLEGE STUDY QUESTIONS

1. What was the command Jesus gave His disciples in Matthew chapter ten? _____

_____

2. Where was the disciples assigned to go? _____

_____

3. They had an assignment to do the following…

(1)_____   (4)_____

(2)_____   (5)_____

(3)_____   (6)_____

4. How many of these manifestations of the kingdom of heaven have you witnessed on a regular basis? _____

5. Jesus prepared His disciples for persecutions. How did Jesus teach we should respond to persecution? _____

_____

_____

6. What did Jesus teach about fear? _____

_____

7. Read Matthew 10:32-33 – Do you find it easy or difficult to witness to those you come in contact with? _____

_____

8. Have the change in your life brought about conflict?

_____

_____

9. What do you think a prophets reward is? _____

_____

10. What is a righteous man's reward? _____
_____

NOTE! Ask your Team Assistant Pastor to give you Scripture for your answers? _____
_____
_____

PREPARE YE THE WAY OF THE LORD

"For this is he that was spoken of by the prophet Esaias, saying, The voice of one crying in the wilderness, Prepare ye the way of the Lord, make his paths straight." (Matthew 3:3)

We are living in the last days. Joel prophesied about the times we are living in almost 835 years before the day of Pentecost came. In Acts 2:15-21, which reads…

> *"For these are not drunken, as ye suppose, seeing it is but the third hour of the day. But this is that which was spoken by the prophet Joel; And it shall come to pass in the last days, saith God, I will pour out of my Spirit upon all flesh: and your sons and your daughters shall prophesy, and your young men shall see visions, and your old men shall dream dreams: And on my servants and on my handmaidens I will pour out in those days of my Spirit; and they shall prophesy: And I will shew wonders in heaven above, and signs in the earth beneath; blood, and fire, and vapour of smoke: The sun shall be turned into darkness, and the moon into blood, before that great and notable day of the Lord come: And it shall come to pass, that whosoever shall call on the name of the Lord shall be saved."*

In the midst of all the trouble and the falling away, the Lord is pouring out His Spirit. There are men and women of God who had been called, anointed and appointed by God to be a voice crying in the wilderness places of the world. The voice must continue to be heard until the Lord returns. ARISE AND PREPARE THE WAY OF THE LORD!

Outreach for Jesus Church & Christian Education Center, Inc.

Pastor Batts is presently teaching from Matthew chapters 5-7 and scriptures from Revelation listed in this book.

If you desire a CD or DVD of these teachings or a list of Pastor Batts' most recent CDs/DVDs and books on Leadership and Christian Growth, you may call our business office Monday-Thursday from 10:00 am to 12:00 noon at (910) 423-2999 or write to the below address and a list of these books, CDs or DVDs will be sent to you.

Outreach for Jesus Church
Attention: Pastor Dorothy Batts
3320 Teakwood Drive
Hope Mills, NC 28348